GU00731372

PROUD TO BE A PROTESTANT!

The Essence of the Protestant Faith

by
Timothy J. E. Cross
B.A.(Hons), B.D.(Hons), Th.D.
Author of *My Father's House, A Postcard from Paul* etc.

Published by
B. McCALL BARBOUR
28 George IV Bridge
Edinburgh EH1 1ES
Scotland

Printed 2003 by
Stanley L. Hunt (Printers) Ltd, Midland Road, Rushden, Northants NN10 9UA

CONTENTS

FOREWORD

One of the greatest tragedies to befall the true Church of Jesus Christ in today's world is the abandonment by many believers of the term *'Protestant'* when publicly declaring their faith. They are ashamed of their *'Protestantism'*, being fearful of appearing bigoted, negative and intransigent in the eyes of those who have embraced the ecumenical and charismatic spirit of the age.

'Proud To Be A Protestant' is a timely publication; clearly defining and expounding the great doctrines of the Faith. This is a work which directs the soul of the reader to the Holy Scriptures and to Christ, the only Mediator between God and men. It is pure, positive *'Protestantism'*, clearly written to address the needs of the saint and the sinner, the simple and the scholarly.

It is my prayer that through this publication many will be called by God the Holy Spirit to the place of repentance and faith in Christ. I also trust that it will be used of the Lord to encourage true Christians to move on with God, unashamed of their ***Protestant Faith***.

SAMUEL R. McKAY
Protestant Truth Society

PREFACE

Protestantism and Biblical Christianity are one and the same. The Protestant Faith is the true Faith – *the Faith once delivered unto the saints* (Jude 3).

The following chapters consist of an explanation of some of the essentials of true Protestantism. Whilst Protestants sometimes disagree on matters of secondary importance, on the great fundamental truths of the Bible they are in complete concord and agreement. This book focuses on those major, foundational Protestant fundamentals on which all Protestants agree.

As the twenty first century goes rapidly on, the tide of secularism seems to have never been higher. It also seems to me that, despite the rapid advancements being made in many areas of life, both the misconceptions about and the misrepresentations of the Protestant Faith are greater now than at any other time in history. The timeliness of this work thus grew on me as the chapters progressed. The current climate has spurred me on to provide a useful and readable 'primer' in Protestantism for my fellow believers. My prayer is that the Lord will use it to give the reader a firmer grounding in our 'like precious Faith.' If, however, the work also proves to attract the curious – those out to enquire as to what Protestants really believe; and if, by the grace of God, this book enables such an one to come to a saving faith in the crucified Saviour, my joy will know no bounds.

I am impelled to express my sincere thanks to those Christian friends who have prayed for me whilst this book was being written. I now cast it on the Lord with the sincere desire that He will use it as a means of His grace, a channel of His truth and an instrument for His greater glory.

But grow in grace and in the knowledge of our Lord and Saviour Jesus Christ. To Him be glory both now and for ever. Amen
(2 Peter 3:18).

TIMOTHY J. E. CROSS
Barry
South Wales

CHAPTER ONE

THE HOLY BIBLE : THE INCOMPARABLE BOOK OF PROTESTANTS

Thy Word is truth (John 17:17).

The Word of our God shall stand for ever (Isaiah 40:8).

For ever, O LORD, Thy Word is settled in heaven (Psalm 119:89).

The Book of Books

'The Bible, and the Bible alone is the religion of Protestants', said William Chillingworth in the 19th century. He was right. The Bible alone is the religion of Protestants because the Bible alone is the Book of God and the God of all books. There is no book like the Bible and there never will be a book that compares with the Bible. The cover of the Bible reads 'Holy Bible.' Holy has been defined variously as 'different, special, of a higher excellence, belonging to God, devoted to God.'

Claiming to possess a Book containing a personal message from the God of the universe might stagger belief – yet this is what Protestants claim. God's Own Book therefore demands our attention like no other. As a message from the God of heaven, woe betide those who ignore it, woe betide those who belittle it, and woe betide any who add to or subtract from its special, significant and saving contents. God's Book, the Bible, is all that we need for a happy life, a happy death and a happy eternity – nothing more, nothing less and nothing else. Article VI of the *39 Articles of Religion* – the subordinate standard of the Church of England – is entitled 'Of the sufficiency of the holy Scriptures for salvation.' It reads as follows:-

Holy Scripture containeth all things necessary for salvation: so that whatsoever is not read therein, nor may be proved thereby, is not to be required of any man, that it should be believed as an article of Faith, or be thought requisite for salvation.

The *Shorter Catechism* opens this way:-

What is the chief end of man?
Man's chief end is to glorify God and to enjoy Him for ever.
What rule hath God given to direct us how we may glorify and enjoy Him?
The Word of God which is contained in the Scriptures of the Old and New Testaments, is the only rule to direct us how we may glorify and enjoy Him.

The Authoritative Book

The question of what is our final authority is more important than we might at first think. We are all actually under authority to a greater or lesser degree. Here in the United Kingdom, we are subject to the laws of the land, and these laws have been carefully framed and written down. On my very first day of employment in my current job with the railways, I was handed a copy of the British Rail 'Rule Book'. Safety is paramount in the railway industry. Employees of the railway cannot do as they please, or dangerous anarchy would ensue. We are all thus bound by the British Rail 'Rule Book' for our own and the public's safety. The 'Rule Book' is the final authority for railway personnel. Going against this book will result eventually in our being dismissed from working for the railways.

When it comes to the vital matter of our soul's eternal well-being though, where do we go to find light – what is our final authority? Answers to this vary from person to person. A Roman Catholic, for instance, considers that the Pope of Rome is an infallible authority on spiritual matters – he declared himself to be so in the late 1800's! For many however, their own whims and wishes are their final authority. They do what they like – and have to live with the personal and social consequences of their actions.

The final and ultimate authority for the Protestant Faith, however, is the Word of God, the Bible. God Himself is the supreme authority.

He is incapable of making mistakes. It follows therefore that His Word is the only infallible, inerrant guide for both our earthly and our eternal well being. The *Westminster Confession* , in chapter one, sections IV and V puts it this way:-

> The authority of the Holy Scripture, for which it ought to be believed, and obeyed, dependeth not upon the testimony of any man, or Church; but wholly upon God (who is truth itself) the author thereof, and therefore it is to be received because it is the Word of God . . .

> the heavenliness of the matter, the efficacy of the doctrine, the majesty of the style, the consent of all the parts, the scope of the whole (which is, to give glory to God), the full discovery it makes of the only way of man's salvation, the many other incomparable excellencies, and the entire perfection thereof, are arguments whereby it doth abundantly evidence itself to be the Word of God.

The Divinely Inspired Book

The Bible – the foundation of the Protestant Faith – is a unique and unparalleled Book in that it claims to be nothing less than the inspired Word of God. It is vital that we understand what Biblical inspiration means, as the divine authority and infallibility of the Scriptures depends on its divine inspiration. To put it bluntly, if the Bible were not divinely inspired, then it would have no more or no less authority than the millions of other books which have been produced over the ages.

In 2 Timothy 3:16,17 we read *All Scripture is given by inspiration of God, and is profitable for doctrine, for reproof, for correction, for instruction in righteousness: That the man of God may be perfect, throughly furnished unto all good works.*

The expression *given by inspiration of God* here is actually just one word in the original. The one word means 'God-breathed.' The Scriptures then are the product of the very breath of God Himself – God's vocalised breath. As words are the vocalised, outward expression of our inner thoughts, the Bible is nothing less than the written expression of the thoughts of God. Almighty God so moved and breathed on the human authors of Scripture – a Moses, a Jeremiah, a John, a Paul, a Peter et al, that He enabled them to communicate His message without error. The Scriptures which these men wrote are the result of Divine inspiration, i.e. the Holy Spirit of God so moved upon the human penmen of the Bible, that they wrote down the exact words of God for the blessing and enlightenment of all who read them. *For the prophecy came not in old time by the will of man: but holy men of God spake as they were moved by the Holy Ghost* (2 Peter 1:21). At this point, it may be helpful to have some precise definitions of Biblical inspiration, as given from the pens of some gifted Protestant theologians:-

B.B. Warfield defines Biblical inspiration as:-

> A supernatural influence exerted on the sacred writers by the Spirit of God, by virtue of which their writings are given Divine trustworthiness.

James Packer defines Biblical inspiration as:-

> A supernatural influence of God's Spirit upon the Biblical authors which ensured that they wrote precisely what God intended them to write for the communication of His truth.

All sixty six books of the Bible therefore have been inspired by God. The Bible is God-breathed from Genesis 1:1 to Revelation 22:21.

Inspiration Illustrated

We hesitate to try and illustrate the miraculous – and the Bible certainly is a miracle Book – but consider for a moment a beautiful piece of classical music, played by a full symphony orchestra. The music was once in the mind of a composer, who then committed it on to paper. Eventually, each individual instrumentalist will play this music in perfect harmony with the others – strings, brass, woodwind and percussion being careful to play what is written, exactly as the composer intended them to play. Each individual player contributes to the harmonious sound of the whole, yet paradoxically, the work, whilst being their work, is in reality the work of the composer.

It is similar with the Bible. Here God used many different human authors, with differing personalities and gifts, living also in different eras of time. Yet each was part of His overall plan of giving to the world His Word. Each played a part in communicating to humanity Himself and His promise and provision for our eternal blessing.

The Gibraltar rock foundation of Protestantism then is the Bible – the divinely inspired Scriptures. Just as Christ's deity was not diminished by His taking upon Himself our humanity, so God's Word is no less diminished by His communication of His Word through the various and varied human authors of Scripture. The divine inspiration of the Scriptures is a key, if not the key doctrine of Protestantism. All else flows and follows on from this. If we are right here we will be right everywhere. True Protestants take their stand on the infallible Book of God. *The grass withereth, the flower fadeth: but the Word of our God shall stand for ever* (Isaiah 40:8).

The Divine Message of the Bible

The sixty six books which comprise the divinely inspired Volume may seem intimidating to some. The Bible certainly is a vast Book, containing many different types of literature between its covers – history, prophecy, poetry, letters, etc. Notwithstanding, the Bible has only one main message: the promise of eternal life in the Lord Jesus Christ. . . . *the holy Scriptures, which are able to make thee wise unto salvation through faith which is in Christ Jesus* (2 Timothy 3:15). John 3:16 actually contains the message of the whole Bible in a nutshell: *God so loved the world, that He gave His only begotton Son, that whosoever believeth in Him should not perish but have everlasting life.*

The Bible alone is a life-giving Book. Peter testified: *Being born again, not of corruptible seed, but of incorruptible, by the Word of God, which liveth and abideth for ever* (1 Peter 1:23). No other book but the Bible can tell us how we can be delivered from the penalty and power of sin, and no other book can tell us how we can enjoy the fellowship with God for which we were designed. The Bible does! It proclaims a *salvation through faith which is in Christ Jesus.*

The Lord Jesus Christ and the Bible are inextricably bound in the believer's personal experience. We can only know Christ if we read the Bible – and when we read the Bible we come face to face with Christ. The Word in print leads us to the Word in Person. The inspired

Word leads us to the incarnate Word, for Jesus Christ is the Word of God made flesh (John 1:14). The Christ in Whom we believe, is the Christ of the Bible.

Practical Implications

Certain implications follow on from the Bible's being the Word of God and proclaiming a salvation to be gained in Jesus Christ. The implication is this: Read the Bible! Heed the Bible! Get to know its contents intimately and submit to it as your binding authority for what you believe and how you behave. God's command to Joshua is also a command to us. *This book of the law shall not depart out of thy mouth; but thou shalt meditate therein day and night, that thou mayest observe to do according to all that is written therein: for then thou shalt make thy way prosperous, and then thou shalt have good success* (Joshua 1:8).

Are you a true Protestant? Do you give the Bible your daily careful and prayerful consideration and meditation? Do you seek the help of God's Spirit – He Who caused the Bible to be written – to enable you to understand and apply the Bible's sacred contents? Is the Bible your daily joy and spiritual food?

The Bible is the foundation of the Protestant Faith. Sola Scriptura – the Bible alone – was the rallying cry of the Protestant Reformation. May it be our rallying cry as well! Well did an anonymous, Bible-loving Christian once write of the Bible:-

> This Book contains the mind of God, the state of man, the way of salvation, the reward of saints and the doom of sinners. Its histories are true, its doctrines holy, its precepts binding. It contains light to direct you, food to support you, comfort to cheer you. It is a traveller's map, the pilgrim's staff, the pilot's compass, the soldier's sword and the Christian's charter. It is a river of pleasure, a mine of wealth, a paradise of glory. Read it to be wise, believe it to be safe, practise it to be holy.

> How precious is the Book divine
> By inspiration given
> Bright as a lamp its doctrines shine
> To guide our souls to heaven

Its light descending from above
Our sin-sick world to cheer
Displays a Saviour's boundless love
And brings His glories near

It shows to man his wandering ways
And where his feet have trod
And brings to view the matchless grace
Of our forgiving God

This lamp through all the tedious night
Of life shall guide our way
Till we behold the clearer light
Of an eternal day.

CHAPTER TWO

THE TRIUNE GOD OF THE BIBLE

Hear, O Israel: The LORD our God is one LORD
(Deuteronomy 6:4).

Go ye therefore and teach all nations, baptising them in the name of the Father and of the Son and of the Holy Ghost
(Matthew 28:19).

The grace of the Lord Jesus Christ and the love of God and the communion of the Holy Ghost, be with you all
(2 Corinthians 13:14).

In complete contrast to all the religions of the world, the Protestant Faith is no mere man-made religion but a God-given revelation. In the Bible, the one, true and living God – the creator and sustainer of all things – has made Himself known. In the Scriptures the otherwise unknowable God has revealed Himself to us. As God's Word, the Bible is nothing less than God's Own revelation of Himself. Apart from this revelation, we would be stumbling in the dark as to God's Person, given to idle speculation and constructing a god in our own image. We would also be completely ignorant as to the way of salvation.

The big question is then begged: What kind of God is revealed to us in the Bible? The answer of Protestantism is: a Triune God. The blessed Trinity describes the God Who is revealed in the Bible – a God Whom we can actually know and love because in His amazing grace He stoops to know, love and eternally bless us. What then do we mean by 'the Trinity'?

1. The Definition of the Trinity

The *Shorter Catechism* asks the question:-

> Are there more Gods than one?

The answer then given is

> There is but One only, the living and true God.

It then goes on to ask:-

> How many persons are there in the Godhead?

The answer given to this is distinctive:-

> There are three persons in the Godhead; the Father, the Son and the Holy Ghost; and these three are one God, the same in substance, equal in power and glory.

When we talk about the Trinity therefore, we are dealing with the paradox that the God of the Bible is Three and the God of the Bible is One. There is only one God, and yet this God exists in the three Persons of Father, Son and Holy Spirit. The Bible reveals that God the Father is God and that the Son is God and that the Holy Spirit is God – yet the Bible is also clear that there are not three Gods, but only one God. We are thus dealing with a deep and profound mystery. This we should expect, for we are finite creatures, and the infinite God can only be above and beyond our limited human minds. This being said, it is yet incumbent on us to grapple with the revelation that God has graciously given to us in the Bible, and to be as clear in our thinking as we can possibly be. This is especially important because all false religions and heresy are a denial of the Trinity in some sense: Roman Catholics, for instance, add a fourth member to the Trinity and worship Mary as if she were God; Islam is adamant that 'God has no Son.' Jehovah's Witnesses deny the deity – the very God-ness – of the Second Person of the Trinity, along with denying that the Holy Spirit is a real person, let alone a Divine Person. All false teaching then is in some way a denial of the Biblical doctrine of the Trinity. This being said though, the actual word 'Trinity' cannot be found in the Bible!

Whilst the word is not found in the Bible though, the doctrine of the Trinity is clearly Biblical. It is there on almost every page. Let us then see that the God Who is revealed in the Bible is a Trinitarian God.

2. The Revelation of the Trinity

i. The Unity of God

That God is One is a basic Biblical axiom. The nearest that the Old Testament gets to a 'Statement of Faith' is Deuteronomy 6:4,5: *Hear, O Israel, the LORD our God, the LORD is One; And thou shalt love the LORD thy God with all thine heart, and with all thy soul, and with all thy might.* This God described here as 'one' is the God of the Bible – and the only God there is. *The LORD is the true God; He is the living God and an everlasting King* (Jeremiah 10:10). As the true God He has no rivals – *I am the LORD, and there is none else, there is no God beside Me* (Isaiah 45:5), and as the true and only God He cannot tolerate idolatry, i.e. worshipping anything or any one other than Himself. The very first commandment states: *I am the LORD thy God . . . Thou shalt have no other gods before Me* (Exodus 20:2,3).

ii. The Tri-unity of God

That God is Three is also plain from the Scriptures. In fact, on the very first page of the Bible we have some hints as to God's Trinity. The opening verse of Genesis states majestically: *In the beginning God created the heaven and the earth* (Genesis 1:1). The Hebrew word for God here is plural – Elohim. A plural of majesty, for sure, but also, in the light of the whole Bible, a plural of Trinity. The creation account next records how God spoke the world into existence. The world was created by His Word. *And God said . . . and it was so* (Genesis 1:3 et al). We know from the New Testament that this creative Word is none less than the Lord Jesus Christ, the Second Person of the Trinity:- *In the beginning was the Word, and the Word was with God, and the Word was God . . . all things were made by Him: and without Him was not anything made that was made . . . And the Word was made flesh and dwelt among us* (John 1:1,3,14). The opening verses of the Bible also refer to the Third Person of the

Trinity, the Holy Spirit, for Genesis 1:2 records how *the Spirit of God moved upon the face of the waters.* All this being so, we can understand how when God created man – the crown of His creation – He did not say 'Let Me make man' but *Let us make man in our image, after our likeness* (Genesis 1:26). The use of 'us' here is certainly a plural of majesty – but in the light of the whole Bible, we cannot rule out a plural of Trinity also.

iii. The Trinity in the New Testament

It is in the New Testament that the Trinity latent in the Old Testament is made patent. Augustine used to say to those who doubted the Trinity 'Go to the Jordan!' By this he meant that the Trinity is clearly seen in the baptism of the Lord Jesus at the River Jordan, at the commencement of His earthly ministry. Taking Luke's account of this, we notice here:-

1. The Second Person of the Trinity: . . . *Jesus also being baptised . . .* (Luke 3:21)
2. The Third Person of the Trinity: *And the Holy Ghost descended in a bodily shape like a dove upon Him . . .* (Luke 3:22)
3. The First Person of the Trinity: *and a voice came from heaven* (God the Father's) *'Thou art My beloved Son, in Thee I am well pleased'* (Luke 3:22).

Then at the end of the Lord Jesus' ministry, His marching, parting orders to His disciples were these: *Go ye therefore and teach all nations, baptising them in the Name* (note 'Name', not 'Names') *of the Father and of the Son and of the Holy Ghost . . .* (Matthew 28:19). It is small wonder then that an early Christian benediction – one still in use today – is Trinitarian. The benediction may be found in 2 Corinthians 13:14: *The grace of the Lord Jesus Christ and the love of God and the communion of the Holy Ghost be with you all.*

3. The Illustration of the Trinity

When we try and illustrate the Triune God of the Bible, in an attempt to make the infinite more comprehensible to our finite minds, we immediately reach a problem: God is beyond illustration. Any 'illustration' of the One worshipped and honoured as *Holy, holy, holy* (Isaiah 6:3) can only fall miserably short of the reality at best, and verge on blasphemous idolatry at worst. Isaac Watts was near the mark when he wrote:-

Almighty God, to Thee
Be endless honours done
The undivided Three
And the mysterious One
Where reason fails, with all her powers
There faith prevails and love adores.

This being said though, we hesitatingly mention some of the illustrations which have been given to try and enable us to understand something of the Triune nature of God.

It has been said that the sun is one, and yet the sun emits light, heat and energy. It has been purported that water can exist, not just as water, but also as ice and steam. It has also been suggested that our human fingers are composed of bone, skin and blood. Most famously, Patrick of Ireland once plucked a three leafed shamrock (the national emblem of Southern Ireland) and said of it 'Three in one.' All of these illustrations though attempt to explain One beyond illustration – the Triune God of the Bible, the God Who is Three and the God Who is One – Three in One and One in Three, Unity in Trinity, Trinity in Unity.

4. The Operation of the Trinity

Astonishingly, the Bible reveals that all three members of the Trinity work in perfect harmony for the salvation of the sinner. That God the holy Trinity stoops to take a saving interest in us staggers belief – but the Bible tells us that it is so. The Bible reveals that each member of the Trinity has a specific and distinct role in line with God's one purpose of procuring our absolute and eternal blessedness.

Writing to some Christians who were going through some perilous times, the apostle Peter yet reminded them that, whilst they may be thought of as less than nothing in the world's eyes, in God's eyes they were actually exceedingly special. Peter opens his first letter by telling those Christians then – and by implication Christians today – that they had been *Elect according to the foreknowledge of God the Father, through sanctification of the Spirit, unto obedience and sprinkling of the blood of Jesus Christ* (1 Peter 1:2). What a Trinitarian verse! It teaches that a true Christian is a Christian because of:-

1. The work of God the Father: in eternity past, in amazing grace, He selected us for eternal salvation in Christ.

2. The work of God the Holy Spirit : for in and of ourselves we are powerless to believe in the Lord Jesus, the Saviour. Those chosen by God the Father in eternity past however will be sanctified – marked out and set apart – in time. He will make us spiritually alive, convict us of our sin, and enable us to avail ourselves personally of the only remedy for our sin, the blood of Jesus. For salvation is equally a result of:-

3. The work of God the Son. Christ shed His blood on Calvary's cross to procure our salvation. Peter's readers would have been well acquainted with the Exodus from Egypt. The Israelites were in peril. The angel of death was passing over their homes. But God provided a way of escape – a salvation. An innocent lamb was to be slain and its blood applied to the doorpost of the home. When God saw the blood of the lamb on the doorpost He withheld His judgment and passed over that blood-stained house. The Holy Spirit enables us to trust the Greater Passover Lamb. He gives us *obedience and sprinkling of the blood of Jesus Christ* i.e. a personal application and appropriation of the redeeming blood of Christ shed for sinners at Calvary.

Salvation then is Trinitarian. The Father elects us for salvation. The Son procured our salvation by shedding His blood and the Spirit applies the procured salvation of Christ personally to our souls. When we think of one Member of the Trinity, we cannot but help think of the Three, for none acts in isolation. The Father sent the Son, and both now send the Holy Spirit. The Holy Spirit leads us to the crucified Christ, and it is the death of Christ which reconciles us to the Father. All three Members of the Trinity then are one in fulfilling God's purpose of grace in our lives. Salvation is Trinitarian, and Christian experience is also Trinitarian. A Christian prays to the Father, and is able to do so because of the merits and mediation of the Son, and a Christian comes to the Father, through the Son, in the power of the

Holy Spirit. Paul could thus write of Christ that *through Him we . . . have access by one Spirit unto the Father* (Ephesians 2:18).

We thus see something of the Trinity in operation. He was active in the creation of the world and He is active in making us into new creations. He is a Saviour God. Knowing this Saviour God and knowing something of the blessing and benefits which God the Holy Trinity brings can only lead to praise. Which brings us to our final point:-

5. The Glorification of the Trinity

True theology – the study of God – can only lead to doxology – ascribing glory to God. A consideration of the mysterious, glorious Trinity – the God of the Bible – can only tax our minds, but it ought also to stir our hearts and impel us to turn aside and worship. The God of the Bible – He Who alone is to be worshipped and adored – is Trinitarian. Christian salvation is Trinitarian. Daily Christian experience is Trinitarian. It comes as no surprise therefore to see that some of the finest Christian hymns have a distinct Trinitarian foundation to them. We will thus end this chapter on a high note, employing again the words of Isaac Watts in ascribing praise to the God of the Bible – the great Three in One and One in Three, Father, Son and Holy Spirit, One God, blessed Trinity:-

We give immortal praise
To God the Father's love
For all our comforts here
And better hopes above
He sent His own eternal Son
To die for sins that man had done

To God the Son belongs
Immortal glory too
Who bought us with His blood
From everlasting woe
And now He lives and now He reigns
And sees the fruit of all His pains

To God the Spirit's name
Immortal worship give
Whose new creating power
Makes the dead sinner live
His work completes the great design
And fills the soul with joy divine

Almighty God to Thee
Be endless honours done
The undivided Three
And the mysterious One
Where reason fails with all her powers
There faith prevails and love adores.

CHAPTER THREE

THE INCOMPARABLE CHRIST OF PROTESTANTISM

Who is the image of the invisible God (Colossians 1:15).

'He that believeth on Me, believeth not on Me, but on Him that sent Me' (John 12:44).

He that honoureth not the Son honoureth not the Father which hath sent Him (John 5:23).

The Protestant Faith and Biblical Christianity are synonymous, and central and integral to Biblical Christianity is a Person – the Person of the Lord Jesus Christ. Christianity is Christ and Jesus Christ is God. *Great is the mystery of godliness: God was manifest in the flesh* (1 Timothy 3:16). Protestantism therefore is taken up with and taken over by the Lord Jesus Christ, in all the glory of His Person and in all the wonder of His saving work.

The Bible and Christ are inextricably bound. If we would know Christ, we must know the Bible, for it is the Scriptures which bear witness to Christ. Paradoxically, both the Bible and Christ are the Word of God. The one is the Word in print and the other is the Word in Person. The Bible is, as we have seen, God's inspired Word. Christ, similarly, is God's incarnate Word – God's Word in the flesh – for *the Word was made flesh and dwelt among us, (and we beheld His glory, the glory as of the only begotten of the Father,) full of grace and truth* (John 1:14). As the incarnate Word, Christ is the unsurpassed revelation of God. *No man hath seen God at any time; the only begotten Son which is in the bosom of the Father, He hath declared Him* (John 1:18).

The Bible and the Christ of the Bible then are central to Protestantism, both being vital for our eternal salvation. We are as totally dependant on the Word in print as we are the Word in Person if we are to enjoy the eternal fellowship with God which is our chief end.

We have entitled this chapter 'The Incomparable Christ of Protestantism.' The big question is 'Where does Christ's incomparability lie?' Of the many answers which could be given, we will focus particularly on the incomparability of His:- conception, conduct, conversation, character, cross, conquest, crowning and coming.

1. Christ's Incomparable Conception

As the eternal Son of God, Christ had no human father. God was His Father. It was fitting therefore that when the eternal Christ entered into this world, He was born of a virgin – the virgin Mary. The Bible is absolutely clear as to Christ's virgin birth – or more correctly, His virginal conception. Matthew's account of Christ's birth at Bethlehem explains carefully how Mary *was found with child of the Holy Ghost* (Matthew 1:18). *Now all this was done, that it might be fulfilled which was spoken of the Lord by the prophet, saying, Behold, a virgin shall be with child, and shall bring forth a son, and they shall call His name Emmanuel, which being interpreted is, God with us* (Matthew 1:22,23).

Luke, with great candour, tells us of Mary's own initial perplexity and puzzlement as to how she could bear a child when she had never been in physical contact with a man. Knowing the facts of life she asked *'How shall this be, seeing I know not a man?'* (Luke 1:34). The explanation given to her by Gabriel, God's messenger, was this: *The Holy Ghost shall come upon thee, and the power of the Highest shall overshadow thee: therefore also that holy thing which shall be born of thee shall be called the Son of God.* (Luke 1:35). Well did an early Christian creed define that Christ was both 'conceived by the Holy Ghost and born of the virgin Mary.' The virgin birth of Christ is fundamental, and there is no alternative to it. Those who arrogantly and blasphemously propose that Christ had a human father will have to follow their own logic and also propose that Christ then inherited his human father's sinful nature. If Christ did inherit our sinful human nature – which in actual fact He did not – then He could not have offered a sinless sacrifice of Himself on the cross to save sinners.

Of course, a virgin birth is not normal. Here however we are dealing with the supra-normal, for in dealing with the incomparable Christ we are dealing with God, and *with God nothing shall be impossible* (Luke 1:37). Consider next:-

2. Christ's Incomparable Conduct

As the birth of Christ was incomparable, so also was His life here on earth as well. No one has ever done the things which Christ did during His three years of public ministry. Where do we begin? Christ was able to raise the dead (John 11, Luke 7:11). Christ was able to walk on water – He walked on the Sea of Galilee, (Matthew 14:25). Christ was able, at a word, to still a storm on the Sea of Galilee (Mark 4:35), so demonstrating His total Lordship over creation. Christ turned water into wine (John 2) and Christ was able to feed five thousand plus, using just five loaves and two fishes (John 6:1). Christ was able to heal the sick instantaneously: He cured Peter's mother-in-law of her fever (Mark 1:29), He cleansed lepers (Mark 1:40), He gave sight to one who was born blind (John 9) and He gave digital dexterity to a man with a withered hand (Mark 3:1). Christ's supernatural power even extended to His being able to cast out demons (Mark 5:1) and so restore peace and equilibrium to the troubled soul. Christ was even able – and is still able – to demonstrate His authority to forgive sins (Mark 2:10) – and *Who can forgive sins but God only?* (Mark 2:7). No life compares with Christ's life – and we have only briefly touched the surface of it. Next we consider:-

3. Christ's Incomparable Conversation

When Christ finished His famous 'Sermon on the Mount', Matthew records that *the people were astonished at His doctrine: For He taught them as one having authority, and not as the scribes* (Matthew 7:28,29). In John 7:46, we see that even Christ's enemies – those who were not out to compliment Him – were forced to admit *Never man spake like this Man.* A perusal of the Gospels forces us to say the same.

Christ's conversation was both astounding, astonishing and outstanding. Consider the wonderful invitation which He gave in Matthew 11:28: *Come unto Me all ye that labour and are heavy laden, and I will give you rest.* Consider His claim to be both the Bread of Life and the provider of the Water of Life (John 6:35 and 7:38). Consider also some of His 'I am' sayings. In John 8:12 Jesus says *I am the light of the world, he that followeth Me shall not walk in darkness, but shall have the light of life.* In John 11:25,26 Jesus makes the claim *I am the resurrection and the life; he that believeth in Me, though he were dead yet shall he live: and whosoever liveth and believeth in Me shall never die.* Then in John 14:6 Jesus states *I am the way, the truth and the life; no man cometh unto the Father, but by Me.* Audacious claims indeed! Truly *Never man spake like this Man.* Such speech is befitting one who is either totally deluded or absolutely divine – a terrible liar or the true Lord. The compelling evidence forces Protestants to have no option but to put Christ into the latter categories. But there is more. Christ was also incomparable in His character:-

4. Christ's Incomparable Character

At both Christ's baptism and His transfiguration, God the Father spoke from heaven and said of Christ *This is My beloved Son, in Whom I am well pleased* (Matthew 3:17 and 17:5).

The most remarkable fact about Christ's character was His total and absolute sinlessness. We are all sinners by nature and practice. We would all be ashamed if all of our public and private thoughts, words and deeds were put under public scrutiny. When Christ issued the challenge *Which of you convinceth Me of sin* (John 8:46), no one was able to answer Him – even though His enemies would dearly have loved to have been able to do so. Scripture is unanimous in bearing witness to the sinlessness of Christ. His character is incomparable as He Himself was and is impeccable. He *knew no sin* (2 Corinthians 5:21). *He did no sin* (1 Peter 2:22). *... in Him is no sin* (1 John 3:5). The latter two testimonies, coming from Peter and John are especially noteworthy. Peter and John were in Christ's special inner circle of disciples. They thus knew Christ more intimately than most. In our world, the closer we get to someone, the more we become aware of their faults, failings and vices – faults, failings and vices that are otherwise hidden from public view. Not so with Christ though. The closer that Peter and John got to Christ, the more convinced they were of His sinless perfection. Christ was without sin. As the sinless One, He alone could offer up Himself as a perfect, spotless, sinless sacrifice to save sinners -*a lamb without blemish and without spot* (1 Peter 1:19). Only a sinless one could save sinners. Such an One was Christ. He was incomparable in His sinless character, as He was also incomparable in His supernatural, saving, sacrificial cross:-

5. Christ's Incomparable Cross

As no one lived like Christ, so also no one died like Christ. His death on the cross was no ordinary death. Crucifixion, gruesome though it was, was a common practice in the Graeco-Roman world of the first century. Christ's death by crucifixion on Calvary's cross was no common death, but a death which procured the salvation of God's people. The eternal Son of God alone was able to offer up His life as an eternal sacrifice for sin, a sacrifice which alone can save all who trust in the crucified Saviour – and save eternally.

> There was no other good enough
> To pay the price of sin
> He only could unlock the gate
> Of heaven and let us in.

Take a careful note of some of the Scriptural explanations of the cross of Christ:-

Once in the end of the world hath He appeared to put away sin by the sacrifice of Himself (Hebrews 9:26).

But this Man (Christ) after He had offered one sacrifice for sins for ever, sat down on the right hand of God (Hebrews 10:12).

Scripture is adamant that Christ's death is incomparable in its saving effects:-

For Christ also hath once suffered for sins, the just for the unjust, that He might bring us to God (1 Peter 3:18).

In Whom we have redemption through His blood, the forgiveness of sins, according to the riches of His grace (Ephesians 1:7).

> Bearing shame and scoffing rude
> In my place condemned He stood
> Sealed my pardon with His blood
> Hallelujah! What a Saviour.

Christ's death however was only one side of the coin of salvation. Romans 4:25 reminds us that Christ *was delivered for our offences, and was raised again for our justification.* Which brings us to:-

6. Christ's Incomparable Conquest

At the heart of Protestantism lies a cross and an empty tomb. The Christ Who died for our sins on the first Good Friday also conquered the grave on the first Easter Sunday. *Whom they slew and hanged on a tree: Him God raised up the third day, and shewed Him openly* (Acts 10:39,40). *He rose again the third day according to the Scriptures* (1 Corinthians 15:4).

The One Who entered into a virgin womb before His birth also exited from a virgin tomb after His death. Christ's incomparable resurrection from the dead brings the many Scriptural evidences for His deity to a climax. He was *declared to be the Son of God with power, according to the Spirit of holiness, by the resurrection from the dead* (Romans 1:4). In His resurrection from the dead we have the final proof-positive that Jesus Christ is God and that His death brings eternal life. Forty days after Christ's resurrection takes us to:-

7. Christ's Incomparable Crowning

Forty days after Christ conquered the grave, He was *received up into glory* (1 Timothy 3:16). The event is known as Christ's 'ascension'. Mark records with great succinctness how *the Lord . . . was received up into heaven, and sat on the right hand of God* (Mark 16:19) – the 'right hand of God' is a place of honour, authority, power and pre-eminence. Luke similarly records that *He was taken up, and a cloud received Him out of their sight* (Acts 1:9).

So just as Christ entered into the world supernaturally, He also departed from the world supernaturally – but here we are dealing with

God, and miracles present no difficulties to omnipotence. What a day it was when Christ returned to glory! Psalm 24:7 gives us a prophetic inkling of it:- *Lift up your heads, O ye gates! and be ye lift up, ye everlasting doors! And the King of glory shall come in.* There in glory, Christ ever lives to intercede for His own (Hebrews 7:25). There in glory, Christ is preparing a home for His own (John 14:1,2). There in glory, Christ receives the worship of heaven and earth. *Worthy is the Lamb that was slain . . .* (Revelation 5:12).

Christ's ascension to heaven and His enthronement in heaven reminds us and reinforces to us that He is King Jesus. *He must reign till He hath put all enemies under His feet* (1 Corinthians 15:25).

> The head that once was crowned with thorns
> Is crowned with glory now
> A royal diadem adorns
> The mighty victor's brow
>
> The highest place that heaven affords
> Is His by sovereign right
> The King of kings, the Lord of lords
> And heaven's eternal light.

Lastly, we notice that the Scriptures also have much to say concerning an event yet to be, namely:-

8. Christ's Incomparable Coming

The Bible is clear that Jesus Christ is coming again. *This same Jesus, Which is taken up from you into heaven, shall so come in like manner as ye have seen Him go into heaven* (Acts 1:11). What a day it will be! And what a contrast there will be between the first and second comings of Christ.

When Christ came the first time, His coming was relatively obscure, noticed only by Mary, Joseph, and some shepherds in an outhouse in Bethlehem. But the Bible tells us that when Christ comes the second time *Behold, He cometh with clouds; and every eye shall see Him, and they also which pierced Him; and all kindreds of the earth shall wail because of Him. Even so. Amen* (Revelation 1:7). At

His trial, the high priest asked Jesus *'Art Thou the Christ, the Son of the Blessed?'* (Mark 14:61). Under oath, the Lord Jesus replied candidly: *'I am; and ye shall see the Son of Man sitting on the right hand of power, and coming in the clouds of heaven'* (Mark 14:62). The apostle Paul explained similarly:*The Lord Himself shall descend from heaven with a shout, with the voice of the archangel, and with the trump of God; and the dead in Christ shall rise first; Then we which are alive and remain shall be caught up together with them in the clouds, to meet the Lord in the air; and so shall we ever be with the Lord* (1 Thessalonians 4:16,17).

So Jesus Christ is certainly coming again. And when He comes again, He will then be manifestly and confessedly seen as the incomparable Christ that He is -*That at the name of Jesus every knee should bow, of things in heaven and things in earth and things under the earth, and that every tongue should confess that Jesus Christ is Lord, to the glory of God the Father* (Philippians 2:10,11).

Protestantism then is centred on a Person – a divine Person, the Lord Jesus Christ. Christ is the Son of God and God the Son. He is the incomparable One as He is the altogether lovely One and the pre-eminent One. Wonder of all wonders though is the fact that this same Christ is also the Saviour and Friend of all who put their faith in Him.

> O, could I speak the matchless worth
> O, could I sound the glories forth
> Which in my Saviour shine!
> I'd soar and touch the heavenly strings
> And vie with Gabriel while he sings
> In notes almost divine.

CHAPTER FOUR

PROTESTANTISM'S REALISTIC VIEW OF THE HUMAN CONDITION

Who can say, 'I have made my heart clean; I am pure from my sin'?
(Proverbs 20:9).

. . . there is no man that sinneth not . . . (1 Kings 8:46).

There is not a just man upon earth that doeth good and sinneth not
(Ecclesiastes 7:20).

Behold, I was shapen in iniquity; and in sin did my mother conceive
me (Psalm 51:5).

The Sad Fact of Human Sin

No one would deny that there is something seriously wrong with the world as it is at the moment. For example, which one of us does not know some very sad, sick, lonely or depressed people? Which one of us does not shudder when we hear some of the local, national or international news? Which one of us is not acquainted with the growing problem of divorce and the painful broken homes and scarred lives which result from it? Which one of us feels safe to walk the streets at night without fear of being attacked? Which one of us would leave our home unlocked at night without fear of being burgled? Which one of us has never experienced a crushing, personal problem? And we could go on . . .

The Protestant Faith is a radical Faith. It goes to the root cause of the wrong both in the world at large and in our own personal world.

Protestantism teaches and preaches that the world is in the state that it is in because of human sin.

It is human sin which has ruined everything. Sin has cut us off from fellowship with God on a 'vertical' level, and the outworking of this is seen on the 'horizontal' level in the disharmony, disorder, degradation, depravity, death and ultimately (apart from God's saving mercy) damnation of which we are all only too well aware.

Protestantism does not bury its head in the sand when it comes to making a diagnosis of the human condition. Protestantism teaches that the root of the problems of the world in which we live is that, by nature, we are separated from God, our Maker – God, the source of all life, love and light. Yes, Protestantism proclaims a wonderful Gospel – the Good News of sins forgiven and peace with God through the Lord Jesus Christ. But the bad news is the necessary backcloth to the Good News, for divine grace makes no sense at all apart from human guilt. We will never see any need for personal conversion to the Saviour, apart from a personal conviction of sin. Without a personal conviction of sin we will remain unaware that we actually need saving. Justification – being declared right with God – is meaningless unless we are convinced that by nature we are not right with God, but that we are sinners under His wrath and condemnation. The Good News of salvation will fall on deaf ears unless we are convinced that we are in desperate need of salvation. Protestantism starts by saying that we desperately need to be saved, for we are sinners by nature and practice – sinners in the hands of an angry God. But how did this perilous state of affairs come about? The Bible alone tells us how.

1. The Roots of Sin

A key 'diagnostic' verse of the Bible is Romans 5:12, which reads: *Wherefore, as by one man sin entered into the world, and death by sin; and so death passed upon all men, for that all have sinned.* The verse tells us that sin originated in our first ancestor, Adam, in the garden of Eden – that garden where perfect fellowship was enjoyed between man and His Maker until sin disrupted it all. Genesis 3 describes how our first ancestors, Adam and Eve, sinned. They disobeyed the plain commandment of God which He had given them.

Their sin of disobedience brought separation and shame on themselves. They fled from their Maker and tried to hide from Him. Their guilt and His righteous anger did not and could not make them feel comfortable in His presence. Notice though that Romans 5:12 also tells us that we are bound up in Adam's sin and guilt. . . . *for that all have sinned.* Adam was what the theologians term our 'federal head'. As his descendants by natural generation, we have inherited his sinful nature. We are all now born with the tendency to sin. We do not have to teach our children how to be naughty. It comes naturally to them. As Adam's descendants, we are sinners by nature and practice. As such we are separated from God our Maker and in need of being reconciled to Him:

> *There is none righteous, no, not one* (Romans 3:10)
> *. . . all have sinned and come short of the glory of God* (Romans 3:23)
> *If we say that we have no sin we deceive ourselves and the truth is not in us* (1 John 1:8).

Protestantism therefore teaches that by nature, humanity, apart from the saving grace of God, is 'fallen' – fallen from fellowship and harmony with God; and, as the *Shorter Catechism* states 'The fall brought mankind into a state of sin and misery.'

Our fallen nature has consequences. It affects our relationship with God and it also affects our relationships with one another. It is noteworthy that after the Fall of Genesis 3, Genesis 4 records the first ever human murder. The loss of a harmonious 'vertical' relationship with God above certainly had and has undesirable consequences on the human, 'horizontal' level:-

2. The Results of Sin

Let us have Romans 5:12 once again: *Wherefore, as by one man sin entered into the world, and death by sin; and so death passed upon all men, for that all have sinned.* Did you notice the sad connection between sin and death? The Bible is crystal clear here. *The wages of sin is death* (Romans 6:23). *Sin, when it is finished, bringeth forth death* (James 1:15). *The soul that sinneth, it shall die* (Ezekiel 18:4). Death is the saddest and most serious of the many consequences of sin, and according to the Bible, death is both physical, spiritual and eternal.

When Adam and Eve sinned, their fellowship with God died a death. Their sin separated them from God – just as our sin separates us from God. *Your iniquities have separated between you and your God, and your sins have hid His face from you* (Isaiah 59:2). Sin results in spiritual death as it also results in physical death. Funerals and graveyards have been a sad fact of life since the Fall – a sadness which will never lessen this side of eternity. Even worse than spiritual and physical death though is eternal death. The Bible sometimes describes this as 'the second death.'

The second death entails being separated from God and under the wrath of God for all eternity. It is this death which is the worst state of all, and this indescribable state is a result of sin – that sin which mars our fellowship with God. Well then does 1 Corinthians 15:56 state that *The sting of death is sin.*

Sin therefore is the root cause of all the human misery in this world and the next. The heart of the problem is the problem of the heart – our sinful, human hearts. The root of the problem is that sin has taken root. The *Shorter Catechism* summarises what we have been saying when it states:-

> All mankind by their fall lost communion with God, are under His wrath and curse and so made liable to all miseries in this life, to death itself, and to the pains of hell for ever.

Thankfully, those who belong to Jesus need never fear the second death, for in dying on the cross for our sins in our place, Jesus took away the sting of death. We will see more of this when we come to consider the cross of Christ, but having considered the sad facts concerning the origin and consequences of sin, let us now consider what the Bible has to say concerning:-

3. The Remedy for Sin

That the Lord Jesus Christ alone is the remedy for sin is fundamental to the Protestant Faith. *Neither is there salvation in any other: for there is none other name under heaven given among men, whereby we must be saved* (Acts 4:12). Protestantism proclaims a Saviour – a Saviour from the penalty and power of sin. That Christ is the answer to our deepest need is the clear and joyful and central testimony of Scripture. Consider the following Scriptures which prescribe Jesus as the remedy for the sad and bad diagnosis of our sin:-

i.   We have seen that sin brings spiritual and physical death – but Jesus brings life: *For the wages of sin is death; but the gift of God is eternal life through Jesus Christ our Lord* (Romans 6:23).

ii. We have seen that sin separates and alienates us from God – but Jesus brings reconciliation to God: *God was in Christ, reconciling the world unto Himself, not imputing their trespasses unto them* (2 Corinthians 5:19). *But now in Christ Jesus ye who sometimes were far off are made nigh by the blood of Christ* (Ephesians 2:13).

iii. Sin makes us unclean. Sin brings personal pollution. Our sinful uncleanness makes us unfit for God's holy presence. *But we are all as an unclean thing, and all our righteousnesses are as filthy rags* (Isaiah 64:6). How good it is to know God's remedy. God's remedy is the blood of Jesus. *The blood of Jesus Christ His Son cleanseth us from all sin* (1 John 1:7).

iv. Sin puts us under the wrath of God – the most fearful reality of all. We *were by nature the children of wrath, even as others* (Ephesians 2:3). A holy God has to punish sin – not to do so would compromise His justice, therefore *It is appointed unto men once to die, but after this the judgment* (Hebrews 9:27). The Bible affirms though that *Jesus . . . delivers us from the wrath to come* (1 Thessalonians 1:10). *For God hath not appointed us to wrath, but to obtain salvation by our Lord Jesus Christ* (1 Thessalonians 5:10). The Bible affirms that Jesus is *the propitiation for our sins* (1 John 2:2) – He appeases the wrath of God. The Bible affirms that, whilst we deserve condemnation, because of the mercy of God in Christ and the work of Christ on the cross, all who belong to Jesus may yet know and rejoice that *There is therefore now no condemnation to them which are in Christ Jesus* (Romans 8:1).

Protestants then take a realistic, Biblical view of humanity. We are sinners. Sin's ravages are with us every day. We have need of a Saviour and Christ is the Saviour for our need. It is this which gives the Protestant Faith an imperative evangelistic incentive. *Believe on the Lord Jesus Christ and thou shalt be saved* (Acts 16:31).

O loving wisdom of our God
When all was sin and shame
A second Adam to the fight
And to the rescue came.

CHAPTER FIVE

THE CENTRALITY OF THE CROSS TO THE PROTESTANT FAITH

And when they were come to the place which is called Calvary there they crucified Him . . . (Luke 23:33).

We preach Christ crucified . . .(1 Corinthians 1:23).

. . . having made peace through the blood of His cross (Colossians 1:20).

The main thesis of the last chapter was that we are sinners under the judgment of God. This being so, we desperately need to be saved. It is here that the Christian Gospel really is good news, for the Christian Gospel may be summarised succinctly in the words *Christ Jesus came into the world to save sinners* (1 Timothy 1:15). Jesus saves! That Jesus is a Saviour Who really saves, is the glory and distinguishing mark of true Protestantism. Whereas Roman Catholicism preaches a human works based 'salvation', i.e. that we must somehow try and save ourselves, Protestantism proclaims a salvation which has already been surely and securely accomplished for us by Christ. The Bible teaches that when Christ died on Calvary's cross, outside the walls of Jerusalem, two thousand years ago, He procured the eternal salvation of all who put their faith in Him. The cross of Christ and the Christ of the cross are the heart of the heart and the centre of the centre of Biblical Christianity. *Christ Jesus came into the world to save sinners* (1 Timothy 1:15), and this wonderful salvation was actually procured for the sinner by Christ's ignominious death by crucifixion on a cruel cross.

We come then to the centrality of the cross to the Christian Faith – often referred to as 'the finished work of Christ' – (c.f. John 19:30). In Galatians 6:14 the apostle Paul wrote *But God forbid that I should glory, save in the cross of our Lord Jesus Christ.* Paul had been saved by the cross, and he never ceased to marvel at it. Desiring to share his experience of the salvation wrought by the cross – the redeeming work of Christ at Calvary – was the supreme motivation behind all of Paul's many and varied missionary labours. The cross was central to his preaching. When he wrote to the church at Corinth, he reminded them of his visit there, and how *I determined not to know any thing among you, save Jesus Christ and Him crucified* (1 Corinthians 2:2).

As the cross was central to the apostle Paul's life and preaching, it is also central and integral to the whole Bible. Open the Bible anywhere, and you will find the cross somewhere. In the Old Testament the cross is prefigured and prophesied. In the Gospels the cross is described. In the Acts the cross is proclaimed. In the New Testament epistles the cross is explained and applied. In the very last book of the Bible, Revelation, the cross is sung about. Revelation records the chorus of the redeemed. The message here rings out loud and clear: *Worthy is the Lamb that was slain* (Revelation 5:12) – slain to save us for all eternity.

The cross of Christ is one of the fundamental fundamentals of the Protestant Faith. Christ's work at Calvary was multi-faceted. A few key words though will enable us to unlock some of the true meaning of the cross of Christ – the cross which is both literally and metaphorically crucial.

1. Substitution

The Bible teaches that when Christ died on the cross, He died in the place of, or in the stead of the sinner. God's ultimate punishment for sin is death. Christ, though, was the only sinless one who has ever lived. Being sinless, He alone was not subject to this death penalty punishment for sin – yet Christ died. When Christ died, therefore, He was not dying for His Own sins but for the sins of others. He died as the sinner's substitute. A selection of key verses will make this plain:-

> *Christ died for our sins* (1 Corinthians 15:3)
> *Who was delivered for our offences* (Romans 4:25)

Christ died for the ungodly (Romans 5:6)
Who His own self bare our sins in His body on the tree (1 Peter 2:24).

Related to Christ's dying as our substitute, is Christ's dying as our:-

2. Propitiation

To propitiate means 'to turn aside the wrath', 'to appease', 'to satisfy' or 'to pacify'. A holy God has to punish sin, for not to do so would compromise His justice. When God's laws are broken, He can only be characterised by righteous indignation. With God, sin has to be punished or justly pardoned.

The wonder of the cross is that it is God's Own way of both punishing sin and pardoning the sinner – *To declare, I say, at this time His righteousness: that He might be just, and the justifier of him which believeth in Jesus* (Romans 3:26). When Christ died on the cross He bore the divine punishment for our sins. By dying on the cross He has eternally turned aside the wrath of God for those who are His. The Gospels record that Christ literally tasted hell on the cross – that most awful final judgment of God, involving being in the eternal outer darkness away from the light of God's presence. In Matthew 27:45,46 we read *Now from the sixth hour there was darkness over all the land unto the ninth hour. And about the ninth hour Jesus cried with a loud voice saying 'Eli, Eli, lama sabachthani?' that is to say 'My God, my God, why hast Thou forsaken Me?'*

A caricature of the doctrine of propitiation pits a stern God the Father against a loving God the Son. Such a caricature betrays an ignorance of what the Bible teaches. The Bible is clear when it teaches that it was the love of God the Father which gave up His Own Son to be the propitiation for our sins. The blessed Trinity always works in total harmony. 1 John 4:10 reads like this: *Herein is love, not that we loved God but that He loved us and sent His Son to be the propitiation for our sins.*

Paradoxically, Calvary was the supreme demonstration of both the love of God and the wrath of God: the wrath of God in punishing sin, and the love of God in pardoning the sinner. *God commendeth His love toward us in that while we were yet sinners Christ died for us* (Romans 5:8).

It is the cross of Christ therefore that turns aside the wrath of God which is our just desert. Sin causes a holy God to be justly angry. We are all sinners. How may we hope to escape from the wrath of God? By trusting in Jesus and His death on the cross for our sins. *He is the propitiation for our sins* (1 John 2:2) – and there is no other. Propitiation then is another key word which unlocks the meaning of the cross.

Jehovah lifted up His rod
O Christ, it fell on Thee
Thou wast sore stricken of Thy God
There's not one stroke for me
Thy tears, Thy blood, beneath it flowed
Thy bruising healeth me

Jehovah bade His sword awake
O Christ, it woke 'gainst Thee
Thy blood the flaming blade must slake
Thy heart its sheath must be
All for my sake, my peace to make
Now sleeps that sword for me.

3. Reconciliation

It is by the cross of Christ that the sinner is reconciled to God. Our sin separates us from God, for He is a God Who is *of purer eyes than to behold evil and canst not look on iniquity* (Habakkuk 3:13). On the cross, in dealing with our sins, Christ dealt with the dreadful barrier which separates and alienates us from God:-

Christ also hath once suffered for sins, the just for the unjust, that He might bring us to God (1 Peter 3:18).

But now in Christ Jesus ye who sometimes were far off are made nigh by the blood of Christ (Ephesians 2:13).

The cross of Christ therefore is a reconciling cross. The God-man's death on the cross brings God and man together. God is at war with sinners, yet the Gospel proclaims Christ as the One *having made peace through the blood of His cross* (Colossians 1:14).

One facet of salvation then, involves God and the sinner being reconciled. Once experienced, this is a never ending source of joy: *we also joy in God through our Lord Jesus Christ, by Whom we have now received the atonement (reconciliation)* (Romans 5:11).

Another way of describing the reconciling death of Christ is by describing it as an 'atoning' death. The death of Christ for our sins achieves 'atonement', which means that God and the sinner, although formerly at odds, are now 'at one' – our sins having been borne away by Christ.

> Near, so very near to God, nearer I cannot be
> For in the Person of His Son, I am as near as He.

4. Redemption

Ephesians 1:7 reads, concerning Christ, that *In Whom we have redemption through His blood, the forgiveness of sins, according to the riches of His grace.* The blood of Christ therefore, shed on the cross, achieves redemption. Redemption means 'freedom' or 'liberty' – freedom from the penalty and power of sin.

The theme of redemption by blood runs right through the Bible. Central to the Old Testament is the Exodus from Egypt. In this dramatic incident, the people of Israel were miraculously freed from cruel slavery in Egypt. This freedom though was only achieved by the shedding and application of the blood of the Passover lamb. The Old Testament exodus – or redemption – here was a foreshadowing of a greater Redemption to come. Central to the New Testament is redemption – freedom from the dreadful condemnation which our sins deserve. This redemption comes to us absolutely freely, yet paradoxically, this redemption was exceedingly costly. The full definition of redemption is 'to set free by paying a price.' The price paid to redeem the sinner was the blood of Christ. Christ's blood was the payment – the ransom price. *Forasmuch as ye know that ye were not redeemed with corruptible things, as silver and gold, from your vain conversation received by tradition from your fathers; but with the precious blood of Christ, as of a lamb without blemish and without spot* (1 Peter 1:18,19). Christ's death on the cross is a liberating death. It frees us from the condemnation which our sins deserve. *There is therefore now no condemnation to them which are in Christ Jesus* (Romans

8:1). *Christ hath redeemed us from the curse of the law being made a curse for us, for it is written 'Cursed is every one that hangeth on a tree'* (Galatians 3:13).

5. Remission

Speaking of His impending death on the cross, whilst instituting a simple memorial meal of it, Christ Himself explained: *This is My blood of the new testament which is shed for many for the remission of sins* (Matthew 26:28). It is through the work of the cross that our sins are forgiven, and the dreadful weight of their guilt taken away from us. In taking our sins upon Himself, Christ bestows on us God's pardon and remission. Sin puts us in God's debt, but on the cross Christ paid the debt in full. Thus the apostle John could write to some Christians *I write unto you little children, because your sins are forgiven you for His name's sake* (1 John 1:12). It is the cross of Christ which cancels the debt we owe to God. Colossians 2:13 explains of it: *having forgiven you all trespasses; blotting out the handwriting of ordinances that was against us, which was contrary to us, and took it out of the way, nailing it to His cross.*

Protestants therefore are not necessarily 'good' people in the eyes of the world, but inside we know that we are a forgiven people, for in the cross of Christ God has pardoned all of our sins. *Once in the end of the world hath He appeared to put away sin by the sacrifice of Himself* (Hebrews 9:26). In all of this we see that Protestantism is true, apostolic Christianity. The so called 'Apostles Creed' contains that wonderful line 'I believe . . . in the forgiveness of sins.'

> My sin – oh the bliss of this glorious thought!
> My sin, not in part, but the whole
> Is nailed to the cross, and I bear it no more
> Praise the Lord, praise the Lord, O my soul!

Interestingly, the New Testament verb 'to forgive' can also be translated as 'to send away.' This reminds us of the 'scapegoat' of Leviticus 16. In a meaningful ceremony here, we read how the High Priest used to place his hands on the head of the goat and confess the people's sins, symbolically transferring them on to the innocent animal. The goat was then sent away into the wilderness. *And the goat shall bear upon him all their iniquities unto a land not inhabited: and he shall let go the goat in the wilderness* (Leviticus 16:22). As the goat was sent away, so was all the guilt of the peoples' sins. It was a dramatic illustration of Psalm 103:12 – *As far as the east is from the west, so far hath He removed our transgressions from us.* The scapegoat was also a clear foreshadowing of the Lord Jesus Christ – the One Who truly 'sends our sins away.' Pointing to the Lord Jesus, John the Baptist proclaimed: *Behold, the Lamb of God, which taketh away the sin of the world* (John 1:29).

6. Purification

Hebrews 1:3 says concerning Christ's death on the cross that *When He had by Himself purged our sins, sat down on the right hand of the Majesty on high.* The verse informs us that Christ's death also deals with the pollution of sin.

The Bible describes our sin as a personal defilement and uncleanness – an uncleanness that makes us unfit for God's presence. Aware of his sin, David once prayed to God: *Wash me throughly from mine iniquity, and cleanse me from my sin* (Psalm 51:2). In Zechariah 13:1 God gave the promise of *a fountain opened . . . for sin and for uncleanness.* With our New Testament hindsight, we know that this promise was fulfilled in the death of the Lord Jesus Christ. At Calvary, John's Gospel relates how *One of the soldiers with a spear pierced His side, and forthwith came there out blood and water* (John 19:34). Here is a fountain filled with blood, it is drawn from Emmanuel's veins. And sinners who plunge beneath its flood lose all their guilty stains! The Bible declares that *The blood of Jesus Christ His Son cleanseth us from all sin* (1 John 1:7).

Conclusion

True Protestants are all united at the foot of the cross. We cannot get more basic and more fundamental than the finished work of Christ at Calvary.

The cross of Christ defines our view of God – His holy nature and His amazing grace both made the cross a necessity. The cross of

Christ defines our view of ourselves – we are sinners who need to be saved. The cross of Christ defines our view of Christ – He alone, as the Son of God, could offer Himself as an eternal, atoning and all sufficient sacrifice to save our souls. The cross of Christ defines our view of salvation – we are saved by trusting the crucified Saviour. The cross of Christ defines our view of the Church – the Church is the community of those saved by the cross.

A true Protestant trusts in the cross of Christ and the Christ of the cross for eternal salvation. A true Protestant glories in the cross. A true Protestant preaches the cross as the sinner's only hope. A true Protestant is and will be eternally grateful and in God's debt for the cross of Christ. *God forbid that I should glory, save in the cross of our Lord Jesus Christ, by Whom the world is crucified unto me, and I unto the world* (Galatians 6:14).

We sing the praise of Him Who died
Of Him Who died upon the cross
The sinner's hope, let men deride
For this we count the world but loss

Inscribed upon the cross we see
In shining letters 'God is love'
He bears our sins upon the tree
He brings us mercy from above.

CHAPTER SIX

THE INDISPENSABLE ROLE OF THE HOLY SPIRIT IN THE PROTESTANT FAITH

It is the Spirit that quickeneth; the flesh profiteth nothing
(John 6:63).

And I will pray the Father, and He shall give you another Comforter, that He may abide with you for ever, even the Spirit of truth . . .
(John 14:16,17).

No man can say that Jesus is the Lord, but by the Holy Ghost
(1 Corinthians 12:3).

The love of God is shed abroad in our hearts by the Holy Ghost which is given unto us (Romans 5:5).

In chapter two we saw that the full-orbed, Biblical doctrine of God is that of the Trinity – there is but one God, Who exists in the three Persons of God the Father, Son and Holy Spirit. Of the three divine Persons of the Trinity, it is the Holy Spirit Who has been, arguably, the most neglected in Christian theology. We cannot, however, dispense with the Holy Spirit. Apart from the Holy Spirit's ministry, we would have no Bible, and apart from the Bible we cannot know God at all. As we shall see, the Holy Spirit is indispensable to Protestantism. The Bible which He caused to be written reveals that apart from the Holy Spirit's ministry in our lives, we would have no Christian conversion and no authentic Christian living. Christian conversion and Christian conduct – both salvation and sanctification – are impossible apart from the work of the Holy Spirit on us and in us. How vital it is then that we know what the Bible teaches about the Person and Work of the Holy Spirit of God.

1. The Role of the Spirit in Christian Conversion

In John 6:63 the Lord Jesus explains *It is the Spirit that quickeneth (gives life), the flesh profiteth nothing.* Similarly in 2 Corinthians 3:6 Paul states . . . *the Spirit giveth life.*

By nature, we are spiritually dead to God – *dead in trespasses and sins* . . . (Ephesians 2:1). Spiritually dead people are no more able to believe than physically dead people are able to breathe! Apart from the Holy Spirit's gracious impartation of the new life of Christ then, we will remain spiritually dead – in our sins and outside of the salvation procured by Christ.

Salvation involves regeneration – being made spiritually alive. It is the Holy Spirit Who imparts this new life personally to us: *He saved us by the washing of regeneration and renewing of the Holy Ghost* (Titus 3:5). Regeneration by the Spirit even precedes saving faith in Christ, for spiritually dead people are unable to believe in Christ, and thus unable to avail themselves of the redemption procured by Christ on Calvary's cross.

True Protestantism humbles like nothing else can. Salvation, according to Protestantism is solely the work of the Triune God, and God is as equally active today in the application of salvation through the Person of His Spirit, as He was two thousand years ago in the accomplishment of salvation in the Person of His Son. The salvation procured by His Son then is applied by the Spirit to the individual soul now, for it is the Holy Spirit Who makes the finished work of Christ in the past effective and effectual in our souls in the present.

Let us allow the *Shorter Catechism* to summarise and clarify what we have stated so far:-

> How are we made partakers of the redemption purchased by Christ?
> We are made partakers of the redemption purchased by Christ, by the effectual application of it to us *by His Holy Spirit.*
>
> How doth the Spirit apply to us the redemption purchased by Christ?
> The Spirit applieth to us the redemption purchased by Christ by working faith in us and thereby uniting us to Christ in our effectual calling.
>
> What is effectual calling?
> Effectual calling is *the work of God's Spirit,* whereby, convincing us of

our sin and misery, enlightening our minds in the knowledge of Christ and renewing our wills He doth persuade and enable us to embrace Jesus Christ, freely offered to us in the Gospel.

Conviction of Sin

Notice that the *Shorter Catechism* states that one of the ministries of the Holy Spirit is that of 'convincing us of our sin and misery.' This takes us to some of the words of the Lord Jesus which He uttered to His disciples in the upper room during the closing stages of His earthly ministry. In the upper room, the Lord Jesus taught much about the ministry of the Holy Spirit, including His role in the conviction of sin. In John 16:7 Jesus explains:- *'Nevertheless I tell you the truth; it is expedient for you that I go away: for if I go not away, the Comforter will not come unto you; but if I depart, I will send Him unto you. And when He is come, He will reprove the world of sin, and of righteousness, and of judgment . . .*

Conviction of sin therefore precedes conversion to the Saviour. God wounds us before He heals us. Apart from a deep awareness of our personal guilt, any talk of divine grace is meaningless. Salvation is salvation from sin, and it is the Holy Spirit Who breaks down our pride and convinces us that we are lost and condemned sinners in God's sight. The bad news comes first before the Holy Spirit shows us the Saviour as the answer to our need, and graciously enables us to put our faith in Him.

A graphic and real life example of conviction of sin occurred on the day of Pentecost. On the day of Pentecost the Holy Spirit caused great multitudes to be convicted of their sin. Acts 2:37 records that when the crowds heard Peter's Holy Spirit anointed preaching *they were pricked in their heart, and said unto Peter and to the rest of the apostles, 'Men and brethren, what shall we do?'* Peter gladly pointed them to the Saviour. Years later the Holy Spirit was at work in the heart of a cruel jailer Acts 16: 30 records him desperately asking Paul and Silas *'Sirs, what must I do to be saved?'* Paul and Silas gladly pointed Him to the Saviour. If we are 'in Christ' then, it is not because of our doing, but because of the gracious work of God's Holy Spirit. Jesus said *No man can come to Me unless the Father Which hath sent Me draw Him* (John 6:44).

The *Westminster Confession* summarises the role of the Holy Spirit in Christian conversion in the best way we have ever read. Chapter X of this reads:-

> All those whom God hath predestinated unto life, and those only, He is pleased, in His appointed and accepted time, effectually to call, by His Word and *Spirit,* (italics author's) out of that state of sin and death, in which they are by nature to grace and salvation, by Jesus Christ; enlightening their minds spiritually and savingly to understand the things of God, taking away their heart of stone, and giving them a heart of flesh; renewing their wills, and, by His almighty power, determining them to that which is good, and effectually drawing them to Jesus Christ, yet so, as they come most freely, being made willing by His grace.
>
> This effectual call is of God's free and special grace alone, not from anything at all foreseen in man, who is altogether passive therein, until, being *quickened and renewed by the Holy Spirit,* (italics author's) he is thereby enabled to answer this call, and to embrace the grace offered and conveyed in it.

The hymn writer put it poetically:-

> Eternal Spirit! we confess
> And sing the wonders of Thy grace
> Thy power conveys our blessings down
> From God the Father and the Son
>
> Enlightened by Thy heavenly ray
> Our shades and darkness turn to day
> Thine inward teachings make us know
> Our danger and our refuge too.

The Holy Spirit then enables us to start out on the Christian path. *No man can say that Jesus is the Lord but by the Holy Ghost* (1 Corinthians 12:3). The Holy Spirit is also, however, responsible for sustaining us on the Christian pathway too. We will only commence the Christian life, and we will only continue on in the Christian life by the gracious help and ministry of the Holy Spirit. This brings us to our second main heading:-

2. The Role of the Spirit in Christian Conduct

The role of the Holy Spirit in Christian living is multi-faceted. The Holy Spirit graciously gives us many gifts. Four of these blessed gifts are as follows:-

i. The Holy Spirit gives us inner strength

Apart from the Holy Spirit's personal indwelling of us, we would never persevere in the Christian way – the opposition of the world, the flesh and the devil would be too great for us. The Bible though assures the Christian that God actually sends His Holy Spirit to indwell these frail bodies of ours to strengthen us on our way and keep us in the Faith. A greater act of divine condescension could not be conceived. 1 Corinthians 6:19 asks the rhetorical question: *Know ye not that your body is the temple of the Holy Ghost which is in you which ye have of God . . .?* 1 John 4:4 assures us *Greater is He that is in you, than he that is in the world.*

It is good to know that we are not asked to live up to our high Christian calling in our own strength. Paul's prayer for the Ephesians was a kind one – one which we would do well to pray for ourselves and our fellow believers. Paul asked God the Father *That He would grant you, according to the riches of His glory, to be strengthened with might by His Spirit in the inner man* (Ephesians 3:16). By His indwelling Holy Spirit, God empowers and enables us to be the people He commands us to be.

ii. The Holy Spirit imparts Christian assurance

Christian assurance is not the prominent issue that perhaps it once was. The Bible however states that we can actually know personally and be personally assured beyond doubt that we are Christ's and thus truly saved. It is the Holy Spirit Who imparts this assurance to us. *The love of God is shed abroad in our hearts by the Holy Ghost which is given unto us* (Romans 5:5). *. . . ye have received the Spirit of adoption, whereby we cry, 'Abba, Father.' The Spirit itself beareth witness with our spirit, that we are the children of God* (Romans 8:15,16).

Possession of – or being possessed by – God's Spirit can be considered as having God's seal or 'trade mark' of authenticity upon us. Ephesians 1:13 states that when we were enabled to believe the Gospel, we were actually *sealed with that Holy Spirit of promise.* Similarly, 2 Corinthians 1:22 states *Who (God) hath also sealed us, and given the earnest (guarantee) of the Spirit in our hearts.*

The Holy Spirit therefore gives us welcome Christian assurance – and assurance is far removed from presumption. This assurance may be a blessing enjoyed by all Christians, not just a special elite. Assurance is not of the essence of the Faith for sure – yet it is surely a blessing which is well worth seeking. Has the Holy Spirit made the promises of the Bible so real to you that you are in no doubt that you are eternally saved?

iii. The Holy Spirit enables us to partake of the means of grace with profit

The normal, every day means of grace for Protestants are reading the Bible and prayer. We read the Bible daily, and hear God speaking to us, we then respond to God by talking to Him in prayer. Even when we partake of these essential spiritual disciplines though, we are not left to muddle through on our own. God grants us the gracious aid of His Holy Spirit.

Reading the Bible

We have already seen that the ultimate Author of Scripture is God the Holy Spirit. Amazingly, the Author Himself comes to our help when we read His Book. Jesus said *the Comforter, which is the Holy Ghost, Whom the Father will send in My name, He shall teach you all things. . .* (John 14:26). *When He, the Spirit of truth is come, He will guide you into all truth* (John 16:13). This promise of the illuminating ministry of the Holy Spirit has most certainly been fulfilled. Paul could say *Now we have received not the spirit of the world, but the Spirit which is of God, that we might know the things that are freely given to us of God* (1 Corinthians 2:12). We should never open our Bibles without first seeking the aid of the Holy Spirit. A good prayer before reading the Bible is 'Spirit of God my teacher be, showing the things of Christ to me.'

Prayer

According to the Lord Jesus, the secret of prayer is prayer in secret. *But thou, when thou prayest, enter into thy closet, and when thou hast shut thy door, pray to thy Father which is in secret; and thy Father which seeth in secret shall reward thee openly* (Matthew 6:6).

Which one of us though does not sometimes find it difficult to pray? Thankfully, we are promised divine help in prayer – none other than the Holy Spirit's blessed aid. *Likewise the Spirit also helpeth our infirmities: for we know not what we should pray for as we ought: but the Spirit itself maketh intercession for us with groanings which cannot be uttered* (Romans 8:26).

iv. The Holy Spirit gradually transforms our characters

We note finally that the Holy Spirit gradually transforms our character more and more into the image of God. The technical term for this is 'sanctification'. The Holy Spirit makes us more and more holy – the Spirit of Jesus makes us more and more Christ-like. Our sanctification will never be perfect in this life, yet we have to admit that a Christ-like life is an exceedingly powerful Christian witness to the secular world around us. It is the Holy Spirit Who makes us more like Jesus. Galatians 5:22 says *the fruit of the Spirit is love, joy, peace, longsuffering, gentleness, goodness, faith, meekness, temperance.* Notice that these lovely qualities are not natural traits but super-natural ones – they are *the fruit of the Spirit.* Surely, when we read these beautiful character traits we thought of Christ – He Who alone manifested the fruit of the Spirit in a perfect way.

We have seen then something of the indispensable role of the Holy Spirit in the Protestant Faith. Apart from His gracious ministry we would neither commence nor continue in the Christian Faith. It is He Who imparts the infinite blessings of God in Christ to us. Yet even this is not His primary role. His primary role is to glorify Christ. Jesus said that *when He, the Spirit of truth is come . . . He shall glorify Me*

(John 16:13,14). Paradoxically, when a sinner is saved and when a Christian lives a life filled with the Holy Spirit of God, glory is brought to Christ our Saviour. Let us then continually seek to *be filled with the Spirit* (Ephesians 5:18). Jesus promised *How much more shall your heavenly Father give the Holy Spirit to them that ask Him?* (Luke 11:13). When God's people are truly filled with God's blessed Holy Spirit, our lives will indeed bring glory to the One Who loved us and gave Himself for us.

CHAPTER SEVEN

JUSTIFICATION BY FAITH : A CARDINAL PROTESTANT TRUTH

Therefore we conclude that a man is justified by faith without the deeds of the law (Romans 3:28).

Therefore, being justified by faith, we have peace with God through our Lord Jesus Christ (Romans 5:1).

. . . not having mine own righteousness, which is of the law, but that which is through the faith of Christ, the righteousness which is of God by faith (Philippians 3:9).

If we were to summarise what a Protestant believes in just three words, we could do so almost perfectly by saying 'justification by faith.' Justification by faith is a cardinal Protestant truth. Justification by faith alone – sola fide – was one of the rallying cries of the Protestant Reformation of the sixteenth century – the greatest revival of Biblical Christianity since the days of the apostles. Justification by faith is also one of the rallying cries of true Protestants today.

A fuller statement concerning justification however would be to state that a Protestant believes that salvation – or justification (being in the right with God) – is by God's grace alone, by faith alone, in Christ alone, to the eternal glory of God alone.

Before proceeding any further, let us have a definition of both 'justification' and 'faith', so we know precisely what we are dealing with when we consider this primary Protestant truth of Justification by faith. We will utilise the *Shorter Catechism's* masterly conciseness once again:

What is Justification?

Justification is an act of God's free grace, wherein He pardoneth all our sins, and accepteth us as righteous in His sight, only for the righteousness of Christ imputed to us, and received by faith alone.

What is faith in Jesus Christ?

Faith in Jesus Christ is a saving grace, whereby we receive and rest upon Him alone for salvation, as He is offered to us in the Gospel.

Justification is a legal term which concerns our standing before God. By nature we are not right with God – we are guilty sinners, under His wrath. The Good News of the Gospel however proclaims a way whereby sinners may be forgiven and declared right with God by God. This way is by faith in Jesus, that is by trusting in Him and His death on the cross to pardon our sins and restore us to a right standing with our Maker. By faith, we receive and embrace Christ as our own, personal Saviour. Our sins are then forgiven, His perfect righteousness is credited to us, and so we are justified – in the right – by Him freely and forever. Justification lies at the heart of the Protestant understanding of Christian salvation:-

> . . . *justified freely by His grace through the redemption that is in Christ Jesus* (Romans 3:24)
> . . . *justified by His blood* (Romans 5:9)
> *Therefore, being justified by faith, we have peace with God through our Lord Jesus Christ* (Romans 5:1).

Justification by faith reinforces the fact that salvation is God's work and not ours. It is the work of God in Christ. All we 'do' is humbly receive it with gratitude – and faith is the human channel by which we receive God's superlative gift of salvation.

Martin Luther and the Protestant Reformation

The issue of justification – how a sinner may be right with God – came especially to the fore at the time of the Protestant Reformation of the sixteen century. The issue is inextricably bound up with the life of Martin Luther – the life of Luther and the Protestant Reformation are almost one and the same.

Martin Luther desired what we all secretly desire. He desired peace with God. A severe continental thunder storm awakened him to his mortality and of having to face his Maker sooner or later. So terrified was he, that he underwent a career change and became a monk. Here he spared no pain and effort in seeking to achieve personal salvation – or the 'salvation' proffered by the Roman Catholic system of the day. The religion of the Pope though did not actually help him at all – in fact, it made him even more unsettled.

Luther confessed every known sin. Luther wrecked his health by fasting. Luther went on 'pilgrimage' to Rome. Luther partook of the 'Mass'. Luther prayed to the 'saints'. Luther prayed to the virgin Mary. Luther paid his penance . . . but it was all to no avail. He knew that there was still a seemingly insurmountable gulf between his own sinful soul and his holy Maker. He knew that in spite of his efforts, he was not right with God – he lacked the necessary righteousness. How could his guilty soul ever be at peace?

Luther's Salvation

Peace however did eventually come to Luther. He eventually did receive the assurance that all was well between him and God. His salvation came through his discovery, acceptance of and belief in the central message of the New Testament – the message of justification by faith.

A kindly elder directed the troubled Luther to the Scriptures. It was whilst reading the Scriptures – Paul's letter to the Romans in particular – that the truth dawned upon Luther's soul that the righteousness which God demands, and the righteousness which we both lack and require, is actually given to us freely by God as a free gift in Christ! Romans 1:16,17 are the keys to Paul's letter to the Romans, and these verses were also to prove to be key verses in Luther's life. The verses read like this:-

For I am not ashamed of the Gospel of Christ: for it is the power of God unto salvation to everyone that believeth, to the Jew first and also to the Greek. For therein is the righteousness of God revealed from faith to faith; as it is written 'The just shall live by faith.'

In believing and accepting these verses, Luther now knew that the salvation he so longed for was not to be achieved but received. It was not a question of human graft but of divine grace. It was not a case of what we do but what Christ has done. Whereas our works are always imperfect, Luther was now dependant upon the perfect life and sacrificial death of the Lord Jesus Christ for his eternal well-being. The verses teach that salvation is not by works but by faith. We cease working and rest on Christ's finished work. Righteousness – being right with God – is attained by trusting in Jesus. All this was a remarkable turning point in Luther's life – as it was also the spark which ignited the Protestant Reformation. The rediscovery of the message of the Bible revealed just how erroneous, ineffectual and un-Biblical the whole Roman Catholic system was. This turning point in Luther's life – not to mention a turning point in the history of the world – is best described by using Luther's own description of it:-

'I greatly longed to understand Paul's epistle to the Romans, and nothing stood in the way but that one expression, "the righteousness of God", because I took it to mean that righteousness whereby God is just and deals justly in punishing the unrighteous. My situation was that, although an impeccable monk, I stood before God as a sinner troubled in conscience, and I had no confidence that my merit would assuage Him. Therefore I did not love a just and angry God, but rather hated and murmured against Him. Yet I clung to dear Paul and had a great yearning to know what he meant.

'Night and day I pondered until I saw the connection between the righteousness of God and the statement "the righteous shall live by faith". Then I grasped that the righteousness of God is that righteousness by which through grace and sheer mercy God justifies us through faith. Thereupon I felt myself reborn and to have gone through open doors into paradise. The whole of Scripture took on a new meaning, and whereas before the "righteousness of God" had filled me with hate, now it became to me inexpressibly sweet in greater love. This passage of Paul became to me a gate to heaven . . .'

Back to the Bible

The Protestant Reformation of the sixteenth century was a revival of Biblical Christianity – a Biblical Christianity which was becoming covered and obscured by many years of unbiblical and extra-biblical

Roman Catholic traditions. Luther's discovery of the message of the Bible changed his life – as it was also to subsequently change the life of the world.

Notice though, that whilst Luther discovered – or re-discovered – the message of justification by faith, in no way could he claim to have invented it. Protestantism in one sense goes back further than the sixteenth century, for Protestantism goes back to the Bible. Justification by faith, the central message of the Bible, may be traced right the way through the sacred pages of the Word of God:-

Abraham

Two thousand years BC takes us back to the time of Abraham. Abraham, the man of faith, was an archetypal Protestant. He was a sinner, saved by faith. Abraham trusted in God and was saved. Genesis 15:6 tells us that Abraham *believed in the LORD; and He counted it to him for righteousness.*

The Prophets

Isaiah 53 gives us the clearest prophecy of Calvary BC. Notice how Isaiah describes the saving work of Christ in verse eleven of this chapter. He states *by His knowledge shall My righteous Servant justify many; for He shall bear their iniquities.* Some years after Isaiah, the prophet Habakkuk taught similarly: *the just shall live by his faith* (Habakkuk 2:4).

The Lord Jesus Himself

With the utmost reverence, when we turn to the pages of the New Testament, we see that the Lord Jesus Christ Himself preached the Protestant Gospel of justification by faith. In Luke 18:9 He told the 'Parable of the Pharisee and the Tax Collector' – the parable of the good man who went to hell and the bad man who went to heaven. The Pharisee's religious world view in this parable bears an uncanny resemblance to that of Roman Catholicism. The Pharisee pleaded his own supposed good works to win God's favour. The tax collector though, aware of his sin, cast himself on God's grace and mercy. He *smote upon his breast, saying 'God be merciful to me a sinner!'* (Luke 18:13). Listen to the way that the Lord Jesus concluded this parable and note the way in which He describes the tax collector's merciful salvation: *I tell you, this man went down to his house justified rather than the other . . .* (Luke 18:14). Justification by God's sheer grace therefore was the Gospel preached by our Lord and Saviour Jesus Christ.

Paul: The Apostle of Justification

It is when we turn to the letters of the Apostle Paul however that we see the doctrine of justification by faith most dominantly. Paul, the one time Pharisee, had also once viewed salvation in terms of striving to please God by strict obedience to the Law of God. On the Damascus road though he was dramatically, drastically and eternally saved by the grace of God in Christ. From then on, the Gospel of salvation by grace alone through faith alone was the main theme of his life and ministry. In perhaps his earliest letter – the epistle to the Galatians – Paul wrote *Knowing that a man is not justified by the works of the law, but by the faith of Jesus Christ, even we have believed in Jesus Christ, that we might be justified by the faith of Christ, and not by the works of the law: for by the works of the law shall no flesh be justified* (Galatians 2:16).

Many years later, Paul's theme was still the same. From a Roman prison cell he explained to the Philippians that his motivation was still to *win Christ and be found in Him, not having mine own righteousness, which is of the law, but that which is through the faith of Christ, the righteousness which is of God by faith* (Philippians 3:9).

Romans: The Epistle of Justification

In the sixteen chapters of Paul's letter to the Romans, the Holy Spirit has bequeathed to us the clearest and most cogent explanation and exposition of the Gospel of justification by faith ever written. It is for this reason – along with Romans' role in the life of Luther – that the epistle to the Romans has always been especially dear to Protestant people. Romans is a book which we cannot read too often or know too well. Romans may be considered as the manifesto of the Protestant Faith. There is just no substitute for knowing this precious epistle, mastering it and being mastered by it. This being said though, Romans 3:23-25 contains a particular 'purple patch' which seems to compress the message of the whole letter into a very short space, and gives us the gist of the whole of Paul's explanation and celebration of the Gospel of justification. Let us then quote Romans 3:23-25 and then offer a brief exposition of the meaning of these vital verses:-

> *For all have sinned and come short of the glory of God, being justified freely by His grace through the redemption that is in Christ Jesus, Whom God hath set forth to be a propitiation through faith in His blood . . .*

The verses summarise much of what we have already said in previous chapters – showing just how central and integral justification is to the Protestant Faith.

i.   Notice that righteousness is desperately needed *For all have sinned and come short of the glory of God.* Our sin condemns us. We have broken God's law and so stand guilty before God's bar of justice. Condemnation is the opposite of justification. By nature we are condemned for *There is none righteous, no, not one* (Romans 3:10).

ii. Notice that the righteousness God demands, amazingly, is the right-eousness which He freely gives – *being justified freely by His grace . . .* Sola gratia! Grace alone. God's grace is His undeserved kindness and unmerited favour. God's grace is by its nature a gracious gift to be received, not a favour to be earned. God's grace sees Him giving everything for nothing to those who do not deserve anything. In amazing grace God bestows salvation on condemned sinners. Grace is almost too good to believe. It is better experienced than described – 'better felt than telt'. Salvation by grace is both a doctrine to believe and a song to be sung. *For by grace are ye saved through faith and that not of yourselves: it is the gift of God, not of works lest any man should boast* (Ephesians 2:8,9).

iii. Notice that God's justifying grace comes to us in and through the Lord Jesus Christ: *through the redemption that is in Christ Jesus, Whom God hath set forth to be a propitiation through faith in His blood* . . . Christ's death on the cross for our sins frees us from sin's condemnation – Calvary is our redemption. Christ's death on the cross for our sins turns away the righteous anger of God which is our due – Calvary is our propitiation. Because Christ has paid the price and the penalty, we have nothing to pay if we are His. Because Christ accepted the full liability for our sins on the cross, God no longer holds us liable for them. Because Christ was condemned in our place, God is able to justly declare us 'not guilty'. If we belong to Jesus, we have good reason to sing:-

> The terrors of law and of God
> With me can have nothing to do
> My Saviour's obedience and blood
> Hide all my transgressions from view

iv. Notice that God's justifying grace in Jesus Christ is received by faith – *faith in His blood* . . . Faith means receiving Jesus. Faith means trusting in Jesus. Faith means believing in Jesus. 'Faith in Jesus Christ is a saving grace whereby we receive and rest upon Him alone for salvation as He is offered to us in the Gospel' says the *Shorter Catechism.* Salvation is by faith alone in Christ alone. Salvation is by grace and salvation is by faith – grace and faith are the two sides of the one coin. Because salvation is by God's grace it can only be by faith.

Justification by faith therefore is the theme of Romans as it is the theme of Protestantism as it is the theme of Biblical Christianity. *Therefore we conclude that a man is justified by faith without the deeds of the law* (Romans 3:28) – or as Luther translated this verse 'Therefore we conclude that a man is justified by faith alone'.

Conclusion

Justification by faith. This is the doctrine which true Protestants believe and love – and this is the doctrine for which true Protestants will contend without compromise.

How many people, four hundred years after the Reformation still actually believe in justification by works? – religious works, charitable works, 'good' works . . . How many, even of those who attend a 'Protestant' church so called, actually believe, not in justification by faith, but 'justification by outward respect and decency'? Just as sadly, how many today even give the eternal welfare of their souls any thought at all? How vital it is therefore that our concept of justification is in line with God's infallible Word, for what the Bible says is so.

Justification by faith is the central tenet of true Protestantism and a key which again unlocks all the main doctrines of the Bible, telling us about God's nature, our nature, the work of Christ, the work of the Holy Spirit, the true Church and much more.

Justification by faith is the doctrine which adds sweetness to life and living as it also adds sweetness to death and dying. It truly warms the heart and cheers the soul like nothing else in all the world. We quote Article XI of the *Thirty Nine Articles of the Church of England* to close this important chapter:-

> We are accounted righteous before God, only for the merit of our Lord and Saviour Jesus Christ by faith, and not for our own works or deservings. Wherefore, that we are justified by faith only is a most wholesome doctrine, and very full of comfort . . .

CHAPTER EIGHT

THE IMPORTANCE OF THE CHURCH TO PROTESTANTS

. . . Christ also loved the church and gave Himself for it that He might sanctify and cleanse it with the washing of water by the Word (Ephesians 5:25,26).

He is the head of the body, the church (Colossians 1:18).

. . . the house of God, which is the church of the living God, the pillar and ground of the truth (1 Timothy 3:15).

The Collective Side of the Christian Faith

In the last chapter we saw that a true Protestant is characterised by personal, saving faith in Christ. Faith is, of course, an individual act. No one else can believe for us – we cannot be saved by proxy. Protestants rejoice in a personal relationship with God through Christ. Whilst faith is an individual act however, the Protestant Faith is not an individualistic Faith. There is a vital collective and corporate facet to true Protestantism, for when we believe in Christ, we are at once united to the body of Christ, the Church (see Ephesians 1:23). The Church is vital to Protestantism. In fact, the Protestant Church, made up of true believers, can claim to be the true catholic, or universal Church – a body which transcends the nations, the denominations and even time itself.

John Calvin (1509-1564) was arguably the most able Protestant theologian who has ever lived. Calvin's *Institutes of the Christian Religion* is one of the most masterly and systematic explanations of

Biblical Christianity ever written. Book IV of this work is entitled 'The Outward Means By Which God Helps Us,' and the first chapter of this is subtitled 'The True Church.' Listen to what Calvin says here concerning the vital importance of the Church to the Christian Faith:-

> We have shown that Christ becomes ours through faith in His Gospel, so that we share in the salvation and eternal joy secured by Him. Our ignorance, laziness and vanity are such that we need a great deal of help to bring us to living faith. We also need to grow in that faith. So God has made sure we have enough encouragement by entrusting His Gospel to the Church. . .
>
> I will begin with the Church, the gathering of God's children, where they can be helped and fed like babies and then guided by her motherly care, grow up to manhood in maturity of faith . . . For those to whom God is Father, the Church must also be mother. This was true under the law, and it is true even after Christ's coming.

The Church Defined

Before we go any further, let us have some definitions of the Church – this body of people saved by faith in Christ, who meet together for worship, fellowship and edification. Article XIX of the *Thirty Nine Articles of the Church of England,* entitled 'Of the Church' defines the Church so:-

> The visible Church of Christ is a congregation of faithful (i.e. believing) men, in which the pure Word of God is preached, and the Sacraments be duly administered according to Christ's ordinance . . .

Chapter XXV of the *Westminster Confession of Faith* – also entitled 'Of the Church' – is somewhat fuller. This states that:-

> The catholic or universal Church, which is invisible, consists of the whole number of the elect, that have been, are, or shall be gathered into one, under Christ the Head thereof; and is the spouse, the body, the fullness of Him that filleth all in all.

The visible Church, which is also catholic or universal under the Gospel (not confined to one nation, as before under the law), consists of all those throughout the world that profess the true religion; and of their children: and is the kingdom of the Lord Jesus Christ, the house and family of God . . .

Unto this catholic, visible Church, Christ hath given the ministry, oracles and ordinances of God, for the gathering and perfecting of the saints, in this life, to the end of the world: and doth, by His own presence and Spirit, according to His promise, make them effectual thereunto . . .

There is no other head of the Church but the Lord Jesus Christ . . .

Even though the Church has, throughout history, been persecuted, ridiculed and seen as an irrelevance by many, there has never yet been a time when there has not been a congregation of true believers on earth. God has kept His Church. We also know from the Bible that there always will be a Church, for the Lord Jesus pronounced *I will build My Church, and the gates of hell shall not prevail against it* (Matthew 16:18).

The Church Pictured

The Church therefore – the community of those who believe in Jesus – reminds us that the Protestant Faith has a distinct corporate side to it; this without discountenancing the vitality of personal faith. The many word pictures which the New Testament uses to describe the Church cast revealing light on the corporate nature of true Christianity. The New Testament describes the Church in various ways:-

i. A Flock

John 10 describes the Church as a flock of sheep. They are sheep who know Christ as the Good Shepherd – the Good Shepherd Who died for them, and the Good Shepherd Who continually cares for them.

ii. A Body

The apostle Paul likens the Church to a body, which has Christ as its head. *Now ye are the body of Christ and members in particular* (1 Corinthians 12:27). *For as the body is one and hath many members, and all the members of that one body, being many, are one body, so also is Christ* (1 Corinthians 12:12). *He is the head of the body, the Church* (Colossians 1:18).

'Body' here speaks of the Church's total dependence on Christ its living head. It also speaks of the vital role and importance of each and every individual member of the Church. Each has its distinctive place and role in contributing to the overall well-being of the whole. A congregation of God's people is characterised by inter-dependence and not independence. *For the body is not one member, but many* (1 Corinthians 12:14).

iii. A Family

1 Timothy 3:15 describes the Church as *the house of God*. The metaphor reminds us that the Church is a family. This family knows God as Father and is united by a common blood tie – the blood tie of the precious blood of Christ. In amazing grace God adopts sinners into His family. Adoption is one of the highest Christian blessings and responsibilities. It is not accidental that 'brother' and 'sister' are common New Testament Christian designations.

iv. A Building

Both Peter and Paul describe the Church as a Temple, with Christ as the pre-eminent corner stone. Their readers would surely have had the magnificent temple building in Jerusalem in mind when they read their words. *Know ye not that ye are the temple of God and that the Spirit of God dwelleth in you?* (1 Corinthians 3:16). The historic Temple at Jerusalem was carefully constructed of many stones. The apostle Peter takes up this imagery and states that individual believers may be likened to the stones which comprise the Church, the true Temple of God. He exhorts his readers *Ye also, as lively stones, are built up a spiritual house, an holy priesthood, to offer up spiritual sacrifices, acceptable to God by Jesus Christ* (1 Peter 2:5). Like the Temple of old, the Church also manifests something of God's glory and presence in the world, for by His Spirit, God presences Himself both in the Church and in the hearts and lives of the individual believers of which the Church is built.

v. An Assembly

The name 'church' or 'ekklesia' means 'an assembly'. Literally, the word means the 'called out ones.' In ancient times a trumpet call gathered the congregation of Israel together. Similarly, the Church today consists of those who have heard and heeded the call of the Gospel. The effectual call of God in the Gospel has united us to both Christ and one another.

vi. A Bride

In 2 Corinthians 11:2 Paul reminds his readers in the Church at Corinth *I have espoused you to one husband, that I may present you as a chaste virgin to Christ.* The picture of the Church as the 'Bride of Christ' is used frequently in the New Testament. It is a very rich metaphor. The main picture though is that of Christ's loving covenantal commitment to His people – and the love and faithfulness which He expects us to reciprocate back to Him in return.

The Activity of the Church

We mentioned earlier that God has seen to it that there has always been a Church on earth. The earliest description of the Church which we have outside of the New Testament comes from the writings of one Justin Martyr in his work entitled *First Apology.* Written back in the second century, its eye-witness account of a Church worship service then is both interesting and instructive. It was an era in which the Church thrived, in spite of persecution from without, and despite not having any specifically set aside buildings in which to meet. Justin relates of a typical weekly service in those days:-

> On the day called Sunday, all who live in cities or in the country gather together in one place, and the memoirs of the apostles (i.e. the gospels) or the writings of the prophets are read, as long as time permits; then, when the reader has ceased, the president verbally instructs, and exhorts to the imitation of these good things. Then, we all rise together and pray, and when our prayer is ended, bread and wine and water are brought, and the president in like manner offers prayers and thanksgivings according to his ability, and the people assent, saying Amen, and there is a distribution to each, and a participation of that over which thanks has been given.

The Church of the New Testament

The earliest ever description of the Church in action may be found in the New Testament. On the Day of Pentecost, fifty days after Christ's resurrection, Luke records in Acts 2 how that Peter preached the Gospel, and by the grace and power of God no less than three thousand people were saved and joined themselves to the Christian community. In Acts 2:42 Luke then notes that these early disciples *continued stedfastly in the apostles' doctrine and fellowship, and in breaking of bread, and in prayers.*

Acts 2:42 gives us four distinctive marks of the true Church of God – even though these four marks overlap somewhat. As these four marks are characteristic of the Church in every age and era, we are compelled to look at them in a little more detail.

i. The True Church Is Characterised By Apostolic Teaching

They continued stedfastly in the apostles' doctrine . . . The Church is actually *built upon the foundation of the apostles and prophets, Jesus Christ Himself being the chief cornerstone* (Ephesians 2:20). The Church of Christ has definite doctrinal foundations. Teaching is thus one of the vital ministries of the Church, for we all need to be firmly grounded in Christian truth. Gifted teachers help us to understand the

Bible better and help us apply its message to our lives. A well taught Christian will be strong in the Faith. Knowing what we believe delivers us from being *tossed to and fro and carried about with every wind of doctrine, by the sleight of men, and cunning craftiness* (Ephesians 4:14).

Teaching and preaching are central in the Church's activity, for *Faith cometh by hearing, and hearing by the Word of God* (Romans 10:17). True preaching is actually Spirit anointed teaching. It involves both the proclamation, explanation and exhortation of Biblical – apostolic – truth. The Church is only as strong or as weak as its preaching. Preaching is God's ordained method of both saving sinners and edifying saints. As the *Shorter Catechism* says

> The Spirit of God maketh the reading, but especially the preaching of the Word an effectual means of convincing and converting sinners, and of building them up in holiness and comfort, through faith unto salvation.

ii. The True Church Is Characterised By Fellowship

They continued stedfastly in the apostles' . . . fellowship. Fellowship almost sums up Church life. The Church is not so much an institution but a fellowship. Fellowship may be defined as 'a sharing, a participation, a communion.' Fellowship is a common sharing and experience of our *common salvation* (Jude 3). Fellowship involves both fellowship with God and with our fellow believers in the things of God. John wrote his first letter with the express purpose *that ye also may have fellowship with us; and truly our fellowship is with the Father and with His Son Jesus Christ* (1 John 1:3).

The Church is therefore a sharing and caring community. Fellowship entails both give and take. Such fellowship – a common joy in God's salvation – is the sweetest of blessings, better experienced than described. No Christian can survive very well without fellowship – it is both a necessity and a luxury.

Blest be the tie that binds
Our hearts in Christian love
The fellowship of kindred minds
Is like to that above

We share our mutual woes
Our mutual burdens bear
And often for the other flows
The sympathising tear

iii. The True Church Is Characterised By Communion

They continued stedfastly in the . . . breaking of bread. The Lord Jesus ordained that the Church should perpetually remember His death by partaking of a very simple meal of bread and wine. The broken bread and the outpoured wine are visible symbols and reminders which enable us to recall and remember how Christ's body was broken and His blood was shed on Calvary's cross for our salvation. The Lord's people thus partake of the Lord's Supper regularly. It is a visible, tangible reminder of the centrality of the cross – *For as often as ye eat this bread and drink this cup, ye do shew the Lord's death till He come* (1 Corinthians 11:26).

In the Lord's Supper – the breaking of the bread – we enjoy sweet communion with both God and one another. The blood of Calvary's cross reconciles both God to man and man to man, and so we all sit as equals around the Lord's table, and partake of a common loaf. It is a foretaste of heaven indeed.

Amidst us our Beloved stands
And bids us view His pierced hands
Points to His wounded feet and side
Blest emblems of the Crucified

What food luxurious loads the board
When at His table sits the Lord!
The wine how rich, the bread how sweet
When Jesus deigns the guests to meet!

iv. The True Church Is Characterised By Prayer

They continued stedfastly . . . in prayers. The spiritual life of the Church is as dependent on prayer as much as the spiritual life of the individual Christian is dependent on prayer. When the Church meets, she prays – and collective prayer is powerful. (c.f. Acts 12:5 *Peter therefore was kept in prison; but prayer was made without ceasing of the church unto God for him*).

Prayer has many facets. The *Shorter Catechism* states these so:-

> Prayer is an offering up of our desires unto God for things agreeable to His will, in the name of Christ, with confession of our sins and thankful acknowledgment of His mercies.

Prayer involves the praise and adoration of God, as well as the confession of that which impedes our fellowship with Him. Prayer involves thanking God for the many temporal and spiritual blessings He sends our way, as it also involves interceding for those in need. Prayer especially involves the plea that God would glorify His great name, and manifest His glory in the salvation of souls and the building of the Church of the Lord Jesus Christ.

The Worship of the Church

If we were to encapsulate the four marks of the Church as seen rom Acts 2:42, we could state that when the Church meets, it meets for Divine worship. The Church is God's Church – *the Church of the living God* (1 Timothy 3:15). To know God is to know His blessings and benefits in Christ, and this in turn can only elicit the heartfelt praise and thanksgiving from the lips of His people. Worship is the highest activity in which we can ever engage, and when the Church meets, it meets to worship God, our Maker and Saviour:-

> Worship is the declaration by the creature of the greatness of his Creator. It is the glad affirmation by the forgiven sinner of the mercy of his Redeemer. *It is the united testimony of an adoring congregation to the perfection of their common Lord.* (italics author's). It is the summit of the service of the angels and the climax of the eternal purpose of God for His people. It is man's supreme goal here and the consummation of his life in heaven (HA Carson).

Conclusion

In this chapter we have glimpsed something of the meaning, joy, thrill, importance and obligation of belonging to the Church. A detached or an unattached Christian is a contradiction in terms. A true Protestant will pledge him or herself to a local, Bible-believing, Gospel-preaching Church, and be there every Sunday without fail. We have no choice. We need the Church and the Church needs us. The Bible gives us the exhortation to *Let us consider one another to provoke unto love and to good works; not forsaking the assembling of ourselves together, as the manner of some is; but exhorting one another: and so much the more, as ye see the day approaching* (Hebrews 10:24,25).

Whatever people say about the Church, she certainly has a glorious future. For one day Christ will come to take His Church – His bride – for Himself. How much then should the life of every Protestant be bound up with *the Church of God which He hath purchased with His Own blood* (Acts 20:28).

We love the place, O God
Wherein Thine honour dwells
The joy of Thine abode
All earthly joy excels

It is the house of prayer
Wherein Thy servants meet
And Thou, O Lord, art there
Thy chosen flock to greet

We love the Word of life
The Word that tells of peace
Of comfort in the strife
And joys that never cease

We love to sing below
Of mercies freely given
But oh we long to know
The triumph song of heaven

Lord Jesus, give us grace
On earth to love Thee more
In heaven to see Thy face
And with Thy saints adore.

CHAPTER NINE

PROTESTANTS BELIEVE IN A HEAVEN TO BE GAINED AND A HELL TO BE SHUNNED

He that believeth on the Son hath everlasting life: and he that believeth not the Son shall not see life; but the wrath of God abideth on him
(John 3:36).

The verse just quoted is a solemn, serious and sobering one. It is crystal clear in informing us of the great difference that there is, and the infinite and eternal difference that there will be between those who belong to the Lord Jesus and those who do not.

The verse is literally a matter of eternal life and eternal death. It tells us in no uncertain terms of the unending life which those who have been saved will enjoy. It also tells us of the unending punishment that the unsaved will just as certainly experience. Those who belong to Jesus are destined for everlasting blessedness. Those who do not are lost, and they are destined for everlasting punishment -*the wrath of God abideth on him.*

Protestants therefore believe that there is most definitely a heaven to be gained and a hell to be shunned. We believe this because the Word of God teaches that it is so: *And this is the record that God hath given to us eternal life, and this life is in His Son. He that hath the Son hath life; and he that hath not the Son of God hath not life* (1 John 5:11,12). Both John 3:36 and 1 John 5:11,12 divide humanity into two categories – the saved and the lost. The contrast between the two categories could not be more stark.

The Saved

If we belong to Jesus, we need never fear the wrath of God, and we need never fear being cast into hell. Our confidence here is based not on wishful thinking, but on the thoroughness of Christ's saving work on the cross, along with the unbreakable promises of God in the Bible. We have the certain *hope of eternal life which God, that cannot lie, promised before the world began; but hath in due times manifested His Word through preaching . . .* (Titus 1:2,3). Jesus Himself promised *Verily, verily I say unto you, he that heareth My Word and believeth on Him that sent Me, hath everlasting life; and shall not come into condemnation, but is passed from death unto life* (John 5:24). Romans 8:1 declares *There is therefore now no condemnation to them which are in Christ Jesus.* Christ was condemned that we might be saved from condemnation. Christ was made liable for our sins that we might be freed from their dreadful liability. It is *Jesus which delivered us from the wrath to come* (1 Thessalonians 1:10).

A Glorious Heaven to be Gained

Believers in the Lord Jesus go to heaven when they die. Heaven is the special dwelling place of God – think of the family prayer which we pray, it begins 'Our Father, Who art in *heaven . . .* Of course, we enjoy fellowship with God now. Our opening verse tells us that we can enjoy eternal life here and now – *He that believeth on the Son hath everlasting life.* Yet in heaven our fellowship with God will be so much greater, richer and fuller. In heaven, our fellowship with God will be unhindered and un-impeded by all that mars it here on earth. Heaven, for the believer, is *to be absent from the body and to be present with the Lord* (2 Corinthians 5:8). Knowing something of the joy of the Lord now, it is small wonder that we have pinings for heaven. Paul spoke for all believers when he testified of *having a desire to depart, and to be with Christ; which is far better* (Philippians 1:23). Jesus promised an un-named, condemned, dying thief who turned to Him – here is a sinner saved by grace if ever there was one – *'Verily I say unto you, today shalt thou be with Me in Paradise'* (Luke 23:45). No greater bliss can be enjoyed than God's Paradise. Paradise will be unalloyed joy – like Eden before the Fall.

What is heaven like?

Our Heavenly Father's House

It may surprise one to know that the Bible, proportionately, does not say a great deal about heaven. It is far more concerned with the way to heaven – by faith in Jesus – than satisfying our curiosity with details about the life to come. From the words of the Lord Jesus though, we know that heaven is home. Heaven is a prepared home for a prepared people. Jesus said to His disciples in the upper room *In My Father's house are many mansions: if it were not so, I would have told you. I go to prepare a place for you. And if I go and prepare a place for you, I will come again, and receive you unto Myself; that where I am, there ye may be also* (John 14:2,3).

Even here on earth we say 'There's no place like home.' Home is where we feel happy, safe and at ease with our surroundings. If this is so on earth, how much happier, safer and more at ease will we be when we dwell in our eternal home in God's house? Sin is such that, even the best of earthly homes get marred by something or other. We therefore almost cannot conceive of the joy of dwelling in God's home, eternally free from all that spoils – free from the sin within and free from the sin without.

Our Heavenly Treasure House

In a brief, tantalising verse, Peter suggests that heaven will be a house of delights. More specifically, he says that heaven is a treasure house, filled with treasures infinitely greater than this world's tainted gold and devalued currency. In a hymn of praise Peter says *Blessed be the God and Father of our Lord Jesus Christ, which according to His abundant mercy hath begotten us again unto a lively hope by the resurrection of Jesus Christ from the dead, to an inheritance incorruptible, and undefiled, and that fadeth not away, reserved in heaven for you* (1 Peter 1:3,4).

> Fading is the worldling's pleasure, all his boasted pomp and show
> Solid joys and lasting treasure, none but Zion's children know.

Whatever Peter meant exactly, we can be sure that in heaven the truth of Psalm 16:11 will be confirmed for ever. *In Thy presence is fullness of joy, at Thy right hand there are pleasures for evermore.*

The Chorus of Heaven

In heaven we will join the blood-washed throng, who worship God free from all weakness and weariness. *Therefore are they before the throne of God, and serve Him day and night in His temple* (Revelation 7:15). In heaven we will join our voices to the song of men and angels and exclaim *Thou art worthy, O Lord, to receive glory and honour and power* (Revelation 4:11). In heaven, recalling that we are there only because of Calvary and the One Who died at Calvary, we will sing as never before *Worthy is the Lamb that was slain* (Revelation 5:12).

> Our God is the end of the journey
> His pleasant and glorious domain
> For there are the children of mercy
> Who praise Him for Calvary's pain.

In heaven, our joy and thanksgiving will be greater than ever before – and it will continue for all eternity. Eternal life is the highest quality and quantity of life possible. *The gift of God is eternal life through Jesus Christ our Lord* (Romans 6:23).

Protestants therefore believe that there is a heaven to be gained, and it is gained by faith in Jesus. *He that believeth on the Son hath everlasting life* (John 3:36). On a solemn note though, we now turn to the second half of our opening verse. It concerns:-

The Unsaved

. . . he that believeth not the Son shall not see life, but the wrath of God abideth on him (John 3:36).

There is a symmetry to John 3:36. It states that the opposite of believing in Jesus is not believing in Him – i.e. a wilful rejection of the salvation He procured at Calvary. Those who do not believe Christ, the verse says, will not enjoy eternal life. No. They will suffer the most terrible reality of all, namely the wrath of God – and that for ever.

Rejecting Jesus means rejecting the only One Who can deliver us from God's wrath. Apart from Jesus there is no hope, for rejecting the sin-bearer will mean that we will have to bear the full brunt of God's anger on our sins ourselves. 2 Thessalonians 1:7 confirms the truth of our verse. In one of the most formidable passages of the New Testament, Paul directs our attention to the time when the Lord Jesus will return to earth: *when the Lord Jesus shall be revealed from heaven with His mighty angels in flaming fire, taking vengeance on them that know not God and that obey not the Gospel of our Lord Jesus Christ. Who shall be punished with everlasting destruction from the presence of the Lord and from the glory of His power . . .*

We have already seen that believers both have eternal life now, and will have eternal life in all its full consummation in the life to come. It is most sobering and fearful to know that the same is true, negatively, of unbelievers. John 3:18 states *He that believeth on Him is not condemned: but he that believeth not is condemned already, because he hath not believed in the name of the only begotten Son of God.* Unbelievers therefore have already been declared guilty, and a dreadful sentence awaits them – eternity in hell – unless they turn and believe in Jesus while they may.

What Is Hell Like?

The New Testament teaches us much about the awful reality of hell. The eternal punishment of those who do not believe in Jesus is a Bible fact that cannot be explained away. It is there in the Bible to warn us. The New Testament uses vivid imagery to describe this dreadful place, but the reality will be infinitely worse than the words used to describe it.

The New Testament warns us about the absolute and final nature of God's judgment on unrepentant sinners by describing hell as, amongst other things:-

Unquenchable fire (Matthew 3:12), *the everlasting fire* (Matthew 18:8), *hell fire* (Matthew 18:9), *outer darkness; there shall be weeping and gnashing of teeth* (Matthew 22:13).

Hell, said the Lord Jesus, is a cursed place *prepared for the devil and his angels* (Matthew 25:41). Hell is . . . *the lake of fire . . . the second death* (Revelation 20:14). The testimony of Scripture is clear when it says that those who have only been born once will die twice; whereas those who have been born twice – born again of the Spirit of God – will mercifully only die once, and so escape the second death.

Back to Calvary

Perhaps the clearest insight into the awfulness of hell is gained from a consideration of the cross of Calvary. Christ died to save us from hell and judgment. On the cross He actually tasted hell and judgment, when He bore our sins in His sinless body and the full force of God's wrath upon Him. Matthew's Gospel records of this epochal moment in time: *Now from the sixth hour there was darkness over all the land unto the ninth hour. And about the ninth hour Jesus cried with a loud voice 'Eli, Eli, lama sabachthani?' that is to say, 'My God, My God, why hast Thou forsaken Me?'* (Matthew 27:45,46).

From Calvary, we see that hell is darkness. From Calvary we see that hell will involve being cast away from the love of the God Who is pure light. From Calvary we see that hell is being eternally separated from God – the God Who is the source of all life, love and light. Hell then is, paradoxically, an eternal death. So terrible is it, that to rescue us from it, Christ had to experience both supernatural darkness and an awful separation from His Father. He went through it all at Calvary, that those who trust in Him may escape from hell, be reconciled to the Father and enjoy the light and joy of heaven for evermore.

Hell is the final curse of God on sinners, but Christ died to save us from it. *Christ hath redeemed us from the curse of the law being made a curse for us, for it is written 'Cursed is every one that hangeth on a tree'* (Galatians 3:13).

> Death and the curse were in our cup
> O Christ, 'twas full for Thee
> But Thou has drained the last dark drop
> 'Tis empty now for me
> That bitter cup, love drank it up
> Now blessing's draught for me

The Holy One did hide His face
O Christ 'twas hid from Thee
Dumb darkness wrapped Thy soul a space
The darkness due to me
But now that face of radiant grace
Shines forth in light on me.

Conclusion

In concluding this most solemn chapter, we state again that Bible-believing Protestants believe that there is, most definitely a heaven to be gained and a hell to be shunned. Eternal destinies are decided in this life by our attitude to the Lord Jesus.

As Jesus appears in your view
As He is beloved or not
So God is disposed to you
And mercy or wrath is your lot.

He that believeth on the Son hath everlasting life: and he that believeth not the Son shall not see life, but the wrath of God abideth on Him (John 3:36). Heaven or hell? Eternal life or eternal loss? Justification or condemnation? Paradise or perdition? Our eternal destiny depends on whether or not we have saving faith in Jesus, the only Saviour of sinners. The evangelistic task therefore could not be more crucial, important, urgent and imperative: *Behold, now is the accepted time; behold, now is the day of salvation* (2 Corinthians 6:2). *Believe on the Lord Jesus Christ and thou shalt be saved* (Acts 16:31).

CHAPTER TEN

PROUD TO BE A PROTESTANT

Earnestly contend for the Faith which was once delivered unto the saints (Jude 3).

But God be thanked, that ye were the servants of sin, but ye have obeyed from the heart that form of doctrine which was delivered you (Romans 6:17).

Neither is there salvation in any other: for there is none other name under heaven given among men, whereby we must be saved (Acts 4:12).

. . . every one with one of his hands wrought in the work, and with the other hand held a weapon (Nehemiah 4:17).

From the previous nine chapters, we have seen that Protestantism and Biblical Christianity are synonymous terms. The Protestant Faith is the true Faith – *the Faith which was once delivered unto the saints* (Jude 3). A true Protestant therefore will gladly concur with Luther's words, spoken when he was on trial for his beliefs at the famous 'Diet of Worms' :-

> 'I cannot withdraw, for I am subject to the Scriptures I have quoted; my conscience is captive to the Word of God. It is unsafe and dangerous to do anything against one's conscience. Here I stand; I cannot do otherwise. So help me God.'

In Summary

Summarising our previous chapters, we state that a true Protestant – like Luther – is indeed subject to both the Word of God and the God of the Word. The Bible and the Bible alone is the religion of Protestants, for the Bible is nothing less than the Word of God written. A true Protestant shuns idolatry in all its forms, and worships the living and true God alone – the God of the Bible, the great Creator and sustainer of heaven and earth, the One revealed as the blessed Trinity in the Persons of God the Father, Son and Holy Spirit. A true Protestant worships and rejoices especially in the Lord Jesus Christ, He Who is the unsurpassed and unsurpassable revelation of God, for in Christ, God became man. Jesus is 'Emmanuel, God with us'. Jesus alone could say *He that hath seen Me hath seen the Father* (John 14:9). A true Protestant also accepts the Bible's verdict on the human condition: we are sinners by nature and by practice. As sinners, we stand guilty and condemned in the sight of a holy God and thus subject to the wrath of God. This being so, how much does a true Protestant rejoice in God's remedy for sin – the sacrificial, substitutionary, saving death of the Lord Jesus on Calvary's cross. A true Protestant surely has the motto *But God forbid that I should glory, save in the cross of our Lord Jesus Christ* (Galatians 6:14). A true Protestant has been drawn by irresistible grace to the foot of the cross for full salvation, and has been enabled by God's Holy Spirit to say 'Nothing in my hand I bring, simply to Thy cross I cling.' Having been led to the cross, a Protestant marvels at the wonderful exchange which occurred there – the sinless One has taken our sins, and we, the guilty ones, have received His perfect righteousness and so are now justified – declared righteous for Christ's sake – before God. By virtue of our being 'in Christ' we are now acceptable and accepted in God's sight. One of the profoundest verses of Scripture puts it like this: *For He hath made Him to be sin for us, Who knew no sin; that we might be made the righteousness of God in Him* (2 Corinthians 5:21). Justification by God's free grace alone, through faith alone, in Christ alone is one of the distinguishing marks of a Bible believing Protestant – and a never ending source of gratitude, wonder and praise, and a great incentive to live a life of Gospel holiness in response to God's goodness received.

Having been justified by faith, a Protestant will surely also seek the company of those of like precious Faith and join a sound, Bible-believing church – that community of sinners saved by God's grace. It is through the varied ministry of the Church that our Faith is sustained, and we *grow in grace and in the knowledge of our Lord and Saviour Jesus Christ* (2 Peter 3:18).

A Bible believing Protestant will also have an eternal perspective, for a true Protestant knows that, by God's grace, the best is yet to be. Whatever our lot in this world, *our light affliction, which is but for a moment, worketh for us a far more exceeding and eternal weight of glory* (2 Corinthians 4:17). A true Protestant has the assurance that heaven is our ultimate home, not because of what we have done, but because of what Christ has done for us. We can thus echo Paul and say *For to me to live is Christ and to die is gain* (Philippians 1:21). One day our Saviour will take us to be with Himself for all eternity. Whilst appreciating the temporal blessings of this world, we yet testify to *having a desire to depart, and to be with Christ; which is far better* (Philippians 1:23). Truly . . . *Eye hath not seen, nor ear heard, neither have entered into the heart of man, the things which God hath prepared for them that love Him* (1 Corinthians 2:9). Our God is *able to keep you from falling and to present you faultless before the presence of His glory with exceeding joy* (Jude 24).

If all the above is true in your personal experience, you too have cause to say that by God's grace you are PROUD TO BE A PROTESTANT.

The Origin of the term 'Protestant'

It is instructive to note the origin of the term 'Protestant.' The term itself originated during the tumultuous times of the Protestant Reformation of the sixteenth century, specifically at the 'Diet of Speirs' in 1529, under the emperor Charles V. Professor AM Renwick in his work *The Story of the Church* explains:-

> The second Diet (Council) of Speirs (1529) decided that the districts which had become Lutheran after the decision of 1526 should remain so, but that the other districts should remain Catholic in perpetuity with no opportunity to introduce Reformed teaching. The evangelical

minority in the Diet protested against the finding, because no Diet has the right to bind the consciences of men in matters of religion. Because of their protest they were called *'Protestants'*, and the origin of the term is worth noting.

SM Houghton in his book *Sketches from Church History* sheds further light on the origin of the term 'Protestant'. Taking us back again to the 'Diet of Speirs' in 1529 he says that here:-

. . . The Emperor demanded unconditional submission to the Papal yoke. The princes were divided; six of them, together with a large number of German cities, declared that in matters concerning the glory of God and the salvation of souls, their consciences required them to reverence God above all, and that it was not possible for them to yield to the Emperor's demands. Because of this protest, they and their followers were called *Protestants*.

Protestant: A 'Negatively Positive' Word

The Negative Side of the Faith

In the popular mind 'Protestant' is a negative term. To protest is normally taken in the sense of protesting against something, i.e. to reprove and remonstrate. It has to be admitted that the Protestant Faith does have this side to it, either explicitly or implicitly. To worship the true God involves condemning idolatry – the worship of false gods. To rejoice in the Bible's way of salvation involves, by implication, reproving those who preach any other way of salvation. We see this illustrated in Paul's hot protest in Galatians 1:8,9. *But though we, or an angel from heaven, preach any other gospel unto you than that which we have preached unto you, let him be accursed. As we said before, so say I now again, if any man preach any other gospel unto you than that ye have received, let him be accursed.* Unpopular though it is in today's religious climate of 'laissez faire', the Bible yet urges us to *earnestly contend for the Faith which was once delivered to the saints* (Jude 3).

The Positive Side of the Faith

Whilst the above is true, we should also remember the other side of the coin. Under the word 'protest' the dictionary first of all has the definition 'to affirm solemnly.' Protestantism is therefore a very positive Faith, even though it is forced to be negative at times.

A true Protestant is not just against religious error, but is also for the truth. That is, a true Protestant is 'pro the testimony.' A true Protestant witnesses to the truth as it is in Jesus. A true Protestant testifies positively to nothing less than the saving grace of God in Christ. A true Protestant is zealous for the true Gospel that *Christ Jesus came into the world to save sinners* (1 Timothy 1:15).

Protestantism through the Ages

True religion therefore has both a negative and a positive side to it. It both protests against error and falsity and it affirms the truth. This has always actually been the case:-

On the negative side, the Old Testament prophets of Israel protested against the worship of and 'ecumenism' with the false gods of the surrounding nations. On the positive side though they also called the people of Israel back to the LORD, the God of their fathers – the God of the creation and the covenant.

In the New Testament epistle to the Galatians, the apostle Paul is negative when he makes a stinging attack on the 'Judaisers' – an incipient form of Roman Catholicism – which preached a false gospel of justification by human effort. Paul condemned this as *another gospel which is not another* (Galatians 1:6,7). But Paul did more than just a negative condemnation. Paul also positively affirmed that *a man is not justified by the works of the law but by the faith of Jesus Christ* (Galatians 2:16).

Even the Lord Jesus Christ Himself had a ministry which was both negative and positive. In Matthew 23:27, for instance, He negatively condemns ritualistic, legalistic, external religion as *whited sepulchres, which indeed appear beautiful outward, but are within full of dead men's bones, and of all uncleanness.* He condemned all religion which was not of God as *teaching for doctrines the commandments of men* (Matthew 15:9). Yet in Matthew 11:28 the Lord Jesus gives the most positive affirmation and invitation to partake of true religion – to partake of Himself: *Come unto Me all ye that labour and are heavy laden, and I will give you rest.*

Protestantism therefore, with both its negative and positive sides, is truly in the 'Apostolic Succession'. Whilst the term 'Protestant' may have originated in the Reformation of the sixteenth century, the spirit of Protestantism goes back further. It goes back to the Bible, the Book of God and God of the Book.

Conclusion

The rallying cry and call of the Protestant Reformation was 'Back to the Bible.' It has often been stated that three short statements encapsulate the Protestant Reformation:-

i.   Sola Scriptura – the Bible alone
ii. Sola Gratia – we are saved by grace alone
iii Sola Fide – we are saved by faith alone, for faith is the channel by which and through which we receive the grace of God in Christ.

Adding to these three statements, we may also say ' Solus Christus' – for Christ alone saves – and this will then lead us in turn to praise and thanksgiving – Soli Deo Gloria – to God alone be the glory. The end of salvation is not actually our eternal blessing – although salvation of course does bring eternal blessing to us. The end of salvation is actually the glory of God. Soli Deo Gloria. *That we should be to the praise of His glory, who first trusted in Christ* (Ephesians 1:12). If Protestant theology does not lead to Protestant doxology – the heartfelt worship of God – it has not reached its true end.

A Closing Challenge

Are you a true Protestant? Has this book described your beliefs and innermost convictions? Are you *ready always to give an answer to every man that asketh you a reason of the hope that is in you* (1 Peter 3:15)? In these days of irreligion, religious confusion, religious apathy, religious hostility and even false religious fanaticism, can you sincerely say that you are of the true Faith and that therefore you are proud to be a Protestant? Can you put your hand on your heart and say with total honesty: PROUD TO BE A PROTESTANT!

Soli Deo Gloria

EPILOGUE

A debtor to mercy alone
Of covenant mercy I sing
Nor fear, with Thy righteousness on
My person and offering to bring
The terrors of law and of God
With me can have nothing to do
My Saviour's obedience and blood
Hide all my transgressions from view

The work which His goodness began
The arm of His strength will complete
His promise is Yea and Amen
And never was forfeited yet
Things future, nor things that are now
Not all things below nor above
Can make Him His purpose forego
Or sever my soul from His love

My name from the palms of His hands
Eternity will not erase
Impressed on His heart it remains
In marks of indelible grace
Yes, I to the end shall endure
As sure as the earnest is given
More happy, but not more secure
The glorified spirits in heaven

(Augustus M Toplady 1740-78)